Cristian Bodor

The Compatibilities in Zodiacs

Contents

Introduction

Once, I have touched also the land of the zodiacs. Then have followed zodiacal books and the internet. My observations on the nature of some persons have been plaited with the readings made. If I have found friends who have had some of the fitted zodiac signs, this is due to fantasy or a circuit of the emitted energy from our organisms, that forms an energetic conscience in the universe, that can make us to choose our friends after the concepts, respectively the zodiacs, read by anyone sometime, and to the hazard. The zodiacal compatibilities are a point of departure to our relations with the others, the specialty books and our life.

The Chinese Zodiac

The Chinese zodiac contains, besides the well known Chinese **year,** also the **month**, the **day** and the Chinese **hour**, these being the **4 pillars** (4 members) that form our personality.

One pillar = the repetitive cycle of 60 binomials (1;2;3…60;1;2;3;…60;1,2…)

One Chinese binomial(in Latin: bi=2, nome=name) = one element + one animal

There are 5 elements(the sky). Each element contains two consecutive animals from the Chinese cycle. The yin(introvert) or yang(extravert) character of the animal imprints the element. The elements symbolize the 5 planets known at the time:

(5 digits/member=limb or the triad head, neck and body and the 4 tripartite members, or in pray)

Jupiter(the tree), Mars(the fire), Saturn(the earth), Venus(the metal), Mercury(the water).

10 elements(10 types of digits or the lateral parts of the digits/member or 2 eyes, 2 ears, 2 nostrils, 2 digestive orifices, 1 excretory orifice and the umbilicus):

5 yang :   **Tree=T   Fire=F   Earth=E Metal=M Water=W (large letters)**

5 yin :   **earth=e   metal=m   water=w   tree=t   fire=f   (little letters)**

12 animals(the Earth). The 12 animals represent the approximate 12 rotations/year of the Moon around the Earth and the pears of axonal cranial symmetrical fascicles, the 4 elongated digits x 3 articulated segments, the 4 members x 3 major articulated segments:

6 yang :   **rat   tiger   dragon   horse   monkey   dog**

6 yin :   **buffalo   pig   rooster   sheep   snake   rabbit**

T, t, F, f, E, e, M, m, W, w

rat, buffalo, tiger, rabbit, dragon, snake, horse, sheep, monkey, rooster, dog, pig.

Yin, the feminism, the woman, and yang, the masculinism, the man, form the human cosmic universe.

Thus 12 animals x 5 elements = 60 binomials (30 days and 30 nights/lunation, ovulation, the digits of the parents and child) =

6 (2 nostrils, 2 ears, 2 eyes, or head, column and 4 members, or 3 parts x 2 types of members, or in pray) x 10

5 x 6 = 30 pairs or teams of a woman and a man																													
1	11	21	31	41	51	37	27	17	7	57	47	3	13	23	33	43	53	59	49	39	29	19	9	5	15	25	35	45	55
26	16	6	56	46	36	2	12	22	32	42	52	48	38	28	18	8	58	4	14	24	34	44	54	10	60	50	40	30	20

Example: the 47 binomial is the Metal dog (dog M).

1 Chinese period = 20 Chinese binomials (Chinese years, months, days, hours)

1 Chinese cycle = 1 Chinese era = 3 Chinese periods = 60 Chinese binomials (15 visible palm and sole articulated segments x 4 members, the approximate 30 pears of spinal axonal symmetrical fascicules)

1 Chinese grand(great) cycle = 3 Chinese cycles = 9 Chinese periods = 180 Chinese binomials

1 Chinese epoch = 20 Chinese great cycles = 60 Chinese cycles = 180 Chinese periods = 3600 Chinese binomials.

The Chinese zodiac has began, if we extend in the past our current calendar, in II-4-2637.

The day is the first that refers itself to the continuing night/day rotator cycle of 24 hours(24 ribs and thoracic axonal fascicules)=12 Chinese hours. Integral family:

the Chinese **year**=our social relations=we,all the years=taking care of the grandparents,old

the Chinese **month** = our activity = we, all the months = taking care of the parents, adults

the Chinese **day**=our conscious=we,all the days=taking care of the sisters,brothers,peer,friends,young

the Chinese **hour** = our unconscious = we, all the hours = taking care of the children, human beings, nature

For the verification of the calculi of the pillars there is, also on the internet, their free automatic calculation, but we have to modify some things (the examples of the calculation of all the pillars), at: www.fourpillars.net/online4p.php
www.chineseastrologyonline.com/CFTCal2.htm

the animals in function of the elements = the binomials = the bible = the biparentalism = the biodiversities = the biocosmology = the numbers

5 Archangels

Animism Islamism Hebraism Christianism Zoroastrianism Hinduism Buddhism Confucianism Shintoism Messianism Totemism Ecumenism Religion

jubilation	meditation	stabilization	evangelization	mundialization
Shahadah	Munz	Sawm	Zacat	Hagim
Genesis	Departure	Leviticus	Numbers	Deuteronomy
east	south	center	west	north
Jupiter	**Mars**	**Saturn**	**Venus**	**Mercury**
giant finger	marker finger	stalactite finger	wedding-ring finger	minute finger

yang binomial	yin binomial	yang binomial	yin binomial	yang binomial	yin binomial	yang binomial	yin binomial	yang binomial	yin binomial
T=Tree	t=tree	F=Fire	f=fire	E=Earth	e=earth	M=Metal	m=metal	W=water	w=water
1. rat	2. buffalo	3. tiger	4. rabbit	5. dragon	6. snake	7. horse	8. sheep	9. monkey	10. rooster
11. dog	12. pig	13. rat	14. buffalo	15. tiger	16. rabbit	17. dragon	18. snake	19. horse	20. sheep
21. monkey	22. rooster	23. dog	24. pig	25. rat	26. buffalo	27. tiger	28. rabbit	29. dragon	30. snake
31. horse	32. sheep	33. monkey	34. rooster	35. dog	36. pig	37. rat	38. buffalo	39. tiger	40. rabbit
41. dragon	42. snake	43. horse	44. sheep	45. monkey	46. rooster	47. dog	48. pig	49. rat	50. buffalo
51. tiger	52. rabbit	53. dragon	54. snake	55. horse	56. sheep	57. monkey	58. rooster	59. dog	60. pig
extravert	introvert	extravert	introvert	extravert	introvert	extravert	introvert	extravert	introvert

10 Angels

west,north,center,south,east,matter,wings and body of the insects,birds,animals,plants,flowers,fruits,legumes,seeds,mafueng,5 appendices with 10 vertices and valleys or lateral segments of the marine star

http://en.wikipedia.org/wiki/Category:Integers

west,north,up,down,south,east,matter,legs or the rayon comb of the insects,digits of the birds,animals,plants,flowers,fruits,legumes,seeds,allium,6 appendices with 12 vertices and valleys or lateral segments of the snow flake crystal

6 Archapostles

The numbers look like the animals

1	2	3	4	5	6	7	8	9	10	11	12
rat	buffalo	tiger	rabbit	dragon	snake	horse	sheep	monkey	rooster	dog	pig
the tail or body of the rat squirrel chipmunk petauristini petaurillus petromural petromus shrew hamster otter raccoon thokya chinchilla coati ratel opossum possum marmot mole jird gerbil dormouse mouse or the bat	the horn of the buffalo bison zimbru marhã uru aurochs ox bour brună brown bull cow calve cattle taurus banteng gnu gaur gestating zebu yak antelope or bovine	the stripes or jaws of the tiger tigress lion leopard panther puma cougar jaguar cheetah lynx or feline	the hare bunny kangaroo mara or the cat tabby pussy moggy tom kitten caracal or catopuma seated on their posterior members	the head and body of the dragon varan comodo chameleon lizard salamander cosymbotus gecko iguana gavial alligator turtle toad frog batrachian whale or crocodile	the partially coiled serpent snail scolopendra centipede millipede myriapod anguis caterpillar worm viper pitviper crotal krait bongar bungar boa cobra chrysopelea anaconda or python	the head and neck of the horse stallion mare foal huțan mustang takhi tarpan ass onager donkey hemion kiang chigetai dziggetai or zebra okapi giraffe	the head and body of the sheep mouflon merinos bârsană țurcană urial argali llama alpaca dromedary camel chiru goat markhor ibex tur bharal rove goural or gazelle	the body and tail or member of the monkey orangutan chimpanzee chimp bonobo gorilla baboon rhesus macaque gibbon simian tamarin marmoset colugo loris lemur tarsier ape or primate	the body and the tail egg or chick of the hen fowl chicken broody sitter cock kiwi poultry bird platypus sparrow penguin pelican tit stork hoopoe dove pigeon skylark guineafowl turkey emu ostrich ema peafowl or pheasant	the ears fangs hair or spines anterior paws of the dingo ciobănesc mioriţelor shepherd dog barker biter bitch cub pup puppy fox zoro vixen panda marten bear badger koala tanuki wolverine urchin hyena jackal coyote or wolf	the snout and fangs of the hog swine sow boar tapir hippopotamus and the excrescences of the warthog phacochoerus or the horns of the rhinoceros or the trump and ivory of the elephant
1. T	2. t	3. F	4. f	5. E	6. e	7. M	8. m	9. W	10. w	11. T	12. t
13. F	14. f	15. E	16. e	17. M	18. m	19. W	20. w	21. T	22. t	23. F	24. f
25. E	26. e	27. M	28. m	29. W	30. w	31. T	32. t	33. F	34. f	35. E	36. e
37. M	38. m	39. W	40. w	41. T	42. t	43. F	44. f	45. E	46. e	47. M	48. m
49. W	50. w	51. T	52. t	53. F	54. f	55. E	56. e	57. M	58. m	59. W	60. w
extravert	introvert	extravert	introvert	extravert	introvert	extravert	introvert	extravert	introvert	extravert	introvert

12 Apostles

The calculation of the binomial of the Chinese solar **year**:
The Chinese solar year begins at February(II) 4 and ends in the next year on February(II) 3.
A part of the Chinese years, already calculated, are in a table at the fengshui chapter.

- **for those born between 2000-2099**, the mathematical formula is:
$2003 \Leftrightarrow 03$(the last two figures of the standard year)+**17**=20 = sheep of water, the Chinese year, those born before II 4 2003 are 20-1=19=horse of Water
Examples:
XII 23 2003$\Leftrightarrow$03+17=20=sheep w, the Chinese year binomial
II 2 2003$\Leftrightarrow$03+17=20,20-1(being before II-4)=19=horse W, the Chinese year binomial

- **for those born between the 1900-1999 years**, the mathematical formula is:
$1970 \Leftrightarrow 70$(the last two ciphers of our standard year)+**37** =107, 107-60(so if the result is bigger than 60, a Chinese cycle, we subtract 60)=47(the one born in 1970 being dog M).
But if he is born in 1970, but before February 4, we subtract 1, because the Chinese solar year lasts till February 3 (including), thus it is 47-1=46=the year of the rooster of earth.
Examples:
XI 22 1986 $\Leftrightarrow$ 86+37=123, 123-60=63, 63-60= 3 = tiger F, Chinese year
XII 1 1950 $\Leftrightarrow$ 50+37=87,   87-60=27= tiger M, Chinese year
VI 25 1946 $\Leftrightarrow$ 46+37=83,   83-60=23= dog F, Chinese year
III 30 1946 $\Leftrightarrow$ 46+37=83,   83-60=23= dog F, Chinese year
II 4 1946 $\Leftrightarrow$ 46+37=83,   83-60=23= dog F, Chinese year
II 3 1946 $\Leftrightarrow$ 46+37=83,   83-1=82, 82-60=22= rooster t, Chinese year
XII 11 1943 $\Leftrightarrow$ 43+37=80,   80-60=20= sheep w, Chinese year

Exception make the historical dates, when all the Chinese pillars can modify themselves too, according to the replacement of the Julian old calendar with the Gregorian current one: the XVI century (1582 Italy, France, Belgium, Nederland, Luxemburg, Switzerland, Germany, Indies, Africa, Portugal, Spain, America, Caribbeans, Islands, 1584 Lithuania, Bohemia, Silesia, Moravia, 1586 Poland, Scandinavia, 1587 Austria, Hungary, Romania, Istria, Slavia, adding 11 days), the XVII century (1605 Canada, 1610 Prussia, Germany, Nederland, Africa, 1682 France, adding 11 days), the XVIII century (1700 Germany, Switzerland, Nederland, Denmark, Norway, Iceland, 1752 Great Britain, Hibernia, Portugal, Spain, Italy, Africa, Persia, India, Australasia, Canada, America, France, 1754 Sweden, Finland, adding 12 days), the XIX century (1824 Australia, 1854 New Zealand, 1867 America, Britain, Persia, India, Indochina, Nederland, France, Africa, 1875 Egypt, 1873 Japan, adding 13 days), the XX century (1912 Albania, 1915-1917 Bulgaria, 1918 Russia, Prussia, Lithuania, Latvia, Estonia, Slavia, Tartary, Japan, 1919-1924 Romania and Yugoslavia, 1923 Greece, 1917-1927 Turkey, 1912-1929 China, Mongolia, adding 14 days), the present century (World), there are also countries that use other calendars too (www.wikipedia.org/wiki/Gregorian_calendar).
Example: III 31 1919 (old style=Julian) in Romania becomes IV 14 1919 (new style= Gregorian)$\Leftrightarrow$ 19+37=56, so for those born before these new dates, 14 days are added to the old style date(so not to the calculi)= sheep e, the Chinese year

-**for those born between 1800-1899**:
II 4 1800$\Leftrightarrow$00(the last two digits of the standard year)+**57**=57=monkey M
Those born in II 3 1800 are the anterior binomial, thus: 57-1=56=sheep e.
For the countries where the Julian calendar was not yet replaced with the Gregorian calendar, 13 days are added to the old Julian date to find out the new Gregorian one.

We find the Chinese **month,** by knowing the Chinese year, from the table:

The binomial of the Chinese solar year: 1,6,11,16,21,26,31,36,41,46,51,56 (T,e)			
The binomial of the Chinese solar **month**	Standard date	The binomial of the Chinese solar **month**	Standard date
3 tiger F	II 4 - III 5	9 monkey W	VIII 8 - IX 7
4 rabbit f	III 6 - IV 4	10 rooster w	IX 8 - X 8
5 dragon E	IV 5 - V 5	11 dog T	X 9 - XI 7
6 snake e	V 6 - VI 5	12 pig t	XI 8 - XII 6
7 horse M	VI 6 - VII 7	13 rat F	XII 7 - I 5
8 sheep m	VII 8 - VIII 7	14 buffalo f	I 6 - II 3

The binomial of the Chinese solar year: 2,7,12,17,22,27,32,37,42,47,52,57 (M,t)			
The binomial of the Chinese solar **month**	Standard date	The binomial of the Chinese solar **month**	Standard date
15 tiger E	II 4 - III 5	21 monkey T	VIII 8 - IX 7
16 rabbit e	III 6 - IV 4	22 rooster t	IX 8 - X 8
17 dragon M	IV 5 - V 5	23 dog F	X 9 - XI 7
18 snake m	V 6 - VI 5	24 pig f	XI 8 - XII 6
19 horse W	VI 6 - VII 7	25 rat E	XII 7 - I 5
20 sheep w	VII 8 - VIII 7	26 buffalo e	I 6 - II 3

The binomial of the Chinese solar year: 3,8,13,18,23,28,33,38,43,48,53,58 (F,m)			
The binomial of the Chinese solar **month**	Standard date	The binomial of the Chinese solar **month**	Standard date
27 tiger M	II 4 - III 5	33 monkey F	VIII 8 - IX 7
28 rabbit m	III 6 - IV 4	34 rooster f	IX 8 - X 8
29 dragon W	IV 5 - V 5	35 dog E	X 9 - XI 7
30 snake w	V 6 - VI 5	36 pig e	XI 8 - XII 6
31 horse T	VI 6 - VII 7	37 rat M	XII 7 - I 5
32 sheep t	VII 8 - VIII 7	38 buffalo m	I 6 - II 3

The binomial of the Chinese solar year: 4,9,14,19,24,29,34,39,44,49,54,59 (W,f)			
The binomial of the Chinese solar **month**	Standard date	The binomial of the Chinese solar **month**	Standard date
39 tiger W	II 4 - III 5	45 monkey E	VIII 8 - IX 7
40 rabbit w	III 6 - IV 4	46 rooster e	IX 8 - X 8
41 dragon T	IV 5 - V 5	47 dog M	X 9 - XI 7
42 snake t	V 6 - VI 5	48 pig m	XI 8 - XII 6
43 horse F	VI 6 - VII 7	49 rat W	XII 7 - I 5
44 sheep f	VII 8 - VIII 7	50 buffalo w	I 6 - II 3

The binomial of the Chinese solar year: 5,10,15,20,25,30,35,40,45,50,55,60 (E,w)			
The binomial of the Chinese solar **month**	Standard date	The binomial of the Chinese solar **month**	Standard date
51 tiger T	II 4 - III 5	57 monkey M	VIII 8 - IX 7
52 rabbit t	III 6 - IV 4	58 rooster m	IX 8 - X 8
53 dragon F	IV 5 - V 5	59 dog W	X 9 - XI 7
54 snake f	V 6 - VI 5	60 pig w	XI 8 - XII 6
55 horse E	VI 6 - VII 7	1 rat T	XII 7 - I 5
56 sheep e	VII 8 - VIII 7	2 buffalo t	I 6 - II 3

The calculation of the Chinese **day** of birth:

- for example:

XII(December)- 14 -1970 ⇔ 14(the number of the standard day) + the number from the table of the standard months + the number from the table of the standard years =14+34+17=65(minus 60, cause this is a Chinese cycle)=> 65-60=5, which is the Chinese day binomial of the dragon of Earth(5. dragon E)

IV-8-1964 ⇔ 8+31(being a bisect year)+45=84, 84-60=24=pig f, the Chinese day

I-13-1940 ⇔ 13+0+39=52=rabbit t, the Chinese day

standard months	I	II	III	IV	V	VI	VII	VIII	IX	X	XI	XII
usual standard year	0	31	59	30	0	31	1	32	3	33	4	34
bisect standard year (1892,1896, 1904, 1908,1912,1916,1920,1924 1928,1932,1936,1940,1944, 1948,1952,1956,1960,1964, 1968,1972,1976,1980,1984, 1988,1992,1996,2000,2004, 2008,2012,2016,2020,2024 2028,2032,2036,2040,2044, 2048,2052,2056,2060,2064, 2068,2072,2076,2080,2084, 2088,2092,2096, 2104, 2108)	0	31	0	31	1	32	2	33	4	34	5	35

standard years	0	1	2	3	4	5	6	7	8	9
189	18	23	28	34	39	44	49	55	0	5
190	10	15	20	25	30	36	41	46	51	57
191	2	7	12	18	23	28	33	39	44	49
192	54	0	5	10	15	21	26	31	36	42
193	47	52	57	3	8	13	18	24	29	34
194	39	45	50	55	0	6	11	16	21	27
195	32	37	42	48	53	58	3	9	14	19
196	24	30	35	40	45	51	56	1	6	12
197	17	22	27	33	38	43	48	54	59	4
198	9	15	20	25	30	36	41	46	51	57
199	2	7	12	18	23	28	33	39	44	49
200	54	0	5	10	15	21	26	31	36	42
201	47	52	57	3	8	13	18	24	29	34
202	39	45	50	55	0	6	11	16	21	27
203	32	37	42	48	53	58	3	9	14	19
204	24	30	35	40	45	51	56	1	6	12
205	17	22	27	33	38	43	48	54	59	4
206	9	15	20	25	30	36	41	46	51	57
207	2	7	12	18	23	28	33	39	44	49
208	54	0	5	10	15	21	26	31	36	42
209	47	52	57	3	8	13	18	24	29	34
210	39	44	49	54	59	5	10	15	20	26

We find the binomial of the **hour**, by knowing the one of the day and by subtracting from the official hour the eventual daylight saving time (each country has a history of its hours), obtaining the standard hour:

The Chinese **day**'s binomial:1,6,11,16,21,26,31,36,41,46,51,56 (T,e)			
Chinese **hour** binomial	Standard hour	Chinese **hour** binomial	Standard hour
1 rat T	24-1	7 horse M	11-13
2 buffalo t	1-3	8 sheep m	13-15
3 tiger F	3-5	9 monkey W	15-17
4 rabbit f	5-7	10 rooster w	17-19
5 dragon E	7-9	11 dog T	19-21
6 snake e	9-11	12 pig t	21-23
		13 rat F	23-24

The Chinese **day**'s binomial:2,7,12,17,22,27,32,37,42,47,52,57 (M,t)			
Chinese **hour** binomial	Standard hour	Chinese **hour** binomial	Standard hour
13 rat F	24-1	19 horse W	11-13
14 buffalo f	1-3	20 sheep w	13-15
15 tiger E	3-5	21 monkey T	15-17
16 rabbit e	5-7	22 rooster t	17-19
17 dragon M	7-9	23 dog F	19-21
18 snake m	9-11	24 pig f	21-23
		25 rat E	23-24

The Chinese **day**'s binomial:3,8,13,18,23,28,33,38,43,48,53,58 (F,m)			
Chinese **hour** binomial	Standard hour	Chinese **hour** binomial	Standard hour
25 rat E	24-1	31 horse T	11-13
26 buffalo e	1-3	32 sheep t	13-15
27 tiger M	3-5	33 monkey F	15-17
28 rabbit m	5-7	34 rooster f	17-19
29 dragon W	7-9	35 dog E	19-21
30 snake w	9-11	36 pig e	21-23
		37 rat M	23-24

The Chinese **day**'s binomial:4,9,14,19,24,29,34,39,44,49,54,59 (W,f)			
Chinese **hour** binomial	Standard hour	Chinese **hour** binomial	Standard hour
37 rat M	24-1	43 horse F	11-13
38 buffalo m	1-3	44 sheep f	13-15
39 tiger W	3-5	45 monkey E	15-17
40 rabbit w	5-7	46 rooster e	17-19
41 dragon T	7-9	47 dog M	19-21
42 snake t	9-11	48 pig m	21-23
		49 rat W	23-24

The Chinese **day**'s binomial: 5,10,15,20,25,30,35,40,45,50,55,60 (E,w)			
Chinese **hour** binomial	Standard hour	Chinese **hour** binomial	Standard hour
49 rat W	24-1	55 horse E	11-13
50 buffalo w	1-3	56 sheep e	13-15
51 tiger T	3-5	57 monkey M	15-17
52 rabbit t	5-7	58 rooster m	17-19
53 dragon F	7-9	59 dog W	19-21
54 snake f	9-11	60 pig w	21-23
		1 rat T	23-24

There are two types of calculation of the Chinese zodiac:

- <u>at the place of birth</u> (we use the standard hour and date from the place of birth)

- <u>at Beijing or any other place</u> (we transform the standard birth hour and date, to the standard hour and date from a meridian)

<u>Discussions</u>:

The solar Chinese <u>year</u> should begin on December the 7th, at the same time with the first <u>monthly</u> animal(the rat) and not in February the 4th. An esoteric explanation that pleads for the commencement of the solar Chinese year on February the 4th is that the tiger represents the beginning of the spring, thus the sprout of the first plants, the rat representing the seeds, also at the Mongols the succession of the 12 animals begins with the tiger.

The Chinese <u>day</u> should begin at the hour 23 at the same time with the rat hours, or at 00, and then the rat <u>hours</u> to be from 00 to 2 at night and thus all the Chinese hours to be shifted with one hour. There is the idea that these can't be changed and that the Chinese day binomial doesn't have to contain the whole rat.

There are also the 60 minutes, which are not included in the Chinese pillars, each minute would be a binomial, the same the 60 seconds and so on, but the moment of birth with such exactness is impossible to be determined, remaining here too the mystery into our life.

The approximate principal time zones on the Globe, on the horizontal we see that before the <u>standard</u> hour **00** is a standard date of birth, and after 00 is another, but for the calculi we use: www.astro.com or maps and tables by years.

Hawaii	Alaska	Los Angeles	Calgary	Chicago	Washington DC	Santiago	Rio de Janeiro	Sandwich	Azores	GMT London	France	Sighetu Marmatiei	Moscow	Oman	Pakistan	Alma Atan	Saigon	Beijing	Tokio	Sidneo	Solomon	New Zealand	Tonga
1	2	3	4	5	6	7	8	9	10	11	12	13	14	15	16	17	18	19	20	21	22	23	00
2	3	4	5	6	7	8	9	10	11	12	13	14	15	16	17	18	19	20	21	22	23	00	1
3	4	5	6	7	8	9	10	11	12	13	14	15	16	17	18	19	20	21	22	23	00	1	2
4	5	6	7	8	9	10	11	12	13	14	15	16	17	18	19	20	21	22	23	00	1	2	3
5	6	7	8	9	10	11	12	13	14	15	16	17	18	19	20	21	22	23	00	1	2	3	4
6	7	8	9	10	11	12	13	14	15	16	17	18	19	20	21	22	23	00	1	2	3	4	5
7	8	9	10	11	12	13	14	15	16	17	18	19	20	21	22	23	00	1	2	3	4	5	6
8	9	10	11	12	13	14	15	16	17	18	19	20	21	22	23	00	1	2	3	4	5	6	7
9	10	11	12	13	14	15	16	17	18	19	20	21	22	23	00	1	2	3	4	5	6	7	8
10	11	12	13	14	15	16	17	18	19	20	21	22	23	00	1	2	3	4	5	6	7	8	9
11	12	13	14	15	16	17	18	19	20	21	22	23	00	1	2	3	4	5	6	7	8	9	10
12	13	14	15	16	17	18	19	20	21	22	23	00	1	2	3	4	5	6	7	8	9	10	11
13	14	15	16	17	18	19	20	21	22	23	00	1	2	3	4	5	6	7	8	9	10	11	12
14	15	16	17	18	19	20	21	22	23	00	1	2	3	4	5	6	7	8	9	10	11	12	13
15	16	17	18	19	20	21	22	23	00	1	2	3	4	5	6	7	8	9	10	11	12	13	14
16	17	18	19	20	21	22	23	00	1	2	3	4	5	6	7	8	9	10	11	12	13	14	15
17	18	19	20	21	22	23	00	1	2	3	4	5	6	7	8	9	10	11	12	13	14	15	16
18	19	20	21	22	23	00	1	2	3	4	5	6	7	8	9	10	11	12	13	14	15	16	17
19	20	21	22	23	00	1	2	3	4	5	6	7	8	9	10	11	12	13	14	15	16	17	18
20	21	22	23	00	1	2	3	4	5	6	7	8	9	10	11	12	13	14	15	16	17	18	19
21	22	23	00	1	2	3	4	5	6	7	8	9	10	11	12	13	14	15	16	17	18	19	20
22	23	00	1	2	3	4	5	6	7	8	9	10	11	12	13	14	15	16	17	18	19	20	21
23	00	1	2	3	4	5	6	7	8	9	10	11	12	13	14	15	16	17	18	19	20	21	22
00	1	2	3	4	5	6	7	8	9	10	11	12	13	14	15	16	17	18	19	20	21	22	23
a	b	c	d	e	f	g	h	a	b	c	d	e	f	g	h	a	b	c	d	e	f	g	h

The same letters represent approximately some geographical longitudinal zones compatible between them, different from the time zones.

The compatibilities of the geographical zones between the meridians 20 and 30 from the North Pole to the South Pole (the compatibilities between the persons are according to the hours of birth, that are dependent to the time zones, so different calculi)		
100-90	**20-30**	**140-150**
Canada (Nunavut, The Islands: Queen Elisabeth Sverdrup, Axel Heiberg, Bathurst, Devon, Prince of Wales, Somerset, King William; Manitoba, Ontario) America (North Dakota, Minnesota, Wisconsin, South Dakota, Iowa, Illinois, Nebraska, Kansas, Missouri, Oklahoma, Arkansas, Texas, Louisiana, Mississippi), Mexico Guatemala Ecuador (Galapagos Islands) Antarctica (Thurston Peninsula, James Ellsworth Land, Queen Maud Mountains) Those 3 geographical zones form an equilateral triangle when are projected on a plan which is parallel with the circle that cuts the Earth at the equator. These are ideal zones between them, because when a zone is in Aries, the second is in Lion and the third in Sagittarius. More exactly 3 meridians are compatible between them when these are situated at 120 degrees.	Norway(Svalbard Islands; Lapland) Sweden (Lapland) Finland Russia Estonia Latvia Lithuania Belarus Poland Slovakia Hungary Ukraine Danistria Bessarabia Romania Serbia Macedonia Cosovo Albania Bulgaria Greece Libya Egypt Chad Sudan Centerafrica Congo Zair Uganda Rwanda Burundi Angola Zambia Zimbabwe Namibia Botswana Swaziland Lesotho Southafrica Antarctica (Belgium Baudouin Region, Norway Wegener Plateau)	Russia (New Siberian Islands; Yakutia, Habarov, Magadan The Islands: Ioni, Sakhalin, Kuril Kunashir, Iturup, Urup) Japan (The Islands: Hokkaido, Honshu, Izu, Ogasawara) America (The Islands: Marianas, Guam) Micronesia Papua New Guinea Australia (Queensland, New South Wales, Victoria, The Islands: King, Fourneaux Furnaces, Tasmania) Antarctica (France Adélie Land, Australia Victoria Land)

The correspondences of the significations											
January	February	March	April	May	June	July	August	September	October	November	December
Aquarius	Fishes	Aries	Taurus	Gemini	Cancer	Lion	Virgin	Libra	scorpion	Sagittarius	Capricorn
Tiger	Rabbit	Dragon	Snake	Horse	Sheep	Monkey	Rooster	Dog	Pig	Rat	Buffalo

Besides the 3 compatible zones, the affinities of any geographical zone, so not of the persons or time zones, are daily for two hours (a Chinese animal), with each of the 360 geographical meridians of the Earth, successively.

İnglând
The time zones from this table are approximately;
it has to be verified always at www.astro.com or on maps of the time zones on years, thus we find exactly the changes for each time and place of birth but also the eventual presence of the summer time, with its duration that has to be calculated (these are different from the geographical meridians)

GMT - 12 hours

America
(The Islands: Howard, Baker, nautical time)

GMT - 11 hours	GMT - 10 hours	GMT - 9 hours 30'	GMT - 9 hours	GMT - 8 hours 30'
America (The Islands: Kingman, Palmyra Atoll, Midway, Jarvis; Samoa Salamasina) Samoa Niue	America (The Islands: Aleutian of Alaska Unalaska, Hawaii, Kure, Johnston Atoll) The Cook Islands New Zealand (Tokelau Islands) France Polynesia: Society's Islands: Îles du Vent Windward Islands: Tahiti, Moorea, Maiao, Meetia Maitea Mehetia Cerro de San Cristobal Boudoir; Leeward Islands Sous-le-Vent: Raiatea, Huahine, Tahaa, Bora Bora, Maupiti; Austral Islands: Tubuai, Bass, Rurutu, Rimatara; Tuamotu Islands : Anaa, Hao, Mataiva, Maria)	France (Polynesia: Marquises Islands Marquesas de Mendoza: Eiao Knox Masse Fremantle Robert, Hatutu Hatutaa, Motu Hatu Iti, Motu Oa, Motu One Îlots du Sable Sand Lincoln, Nuku Hiva Hova Marchand Madison, Ua Pou Pu Adams, Ua Huka Huahuna Riou Solide Washington, Fatu Hova Hiva Iva Magdalena, Fatu Huku, Hiva Oa Hiwa Hoa Hiavaoa Dominica Dominique, Haava, Moho Tane Motane Molopu San Pedro, Motu Nao Ariane, Terihi, Tahuata Santa Cristina Christine Cristhina Cristana Christana Cristiana Christhiana)	America (the majority of Alaska, AK: Fairbanks, Nome, Anchorage, Palmer, Kenai, Bethel, Homer, Barrow, Seward, Valdez, Stewart, Wassila, Ketchikan, North Pole, Dillingham, Sitka, Cordova, Hooper Bay, Kotzebue, Haines, Petersburg, Houston, Craig, Skagway, Kodiak, Soldotna, Juneau) France (Polynesia: Gambier Islands: Mangareva, Taravai, Aukena, Totegegie, Kamaka, Motu Teiku, Tepapuri, Akamaru, Tarauru, Atumata, Rumarei, Mekiro, Makaroa, Tenoko, Tauna, Tekava)	Britain (Pitcairn Islands)

GMT - 8 hours

Canada
(Yukon:YK:Dawson,Whitehorse;British Columbia,BC:Bennett,Fort Nelson,Kitimat,Prince George,Queen Charlotte,Kamloops,Vancouver,Victoria)

America
(north Idaho,ID:Spokane Kellogg,Coeur d'Allene;Washington,WA:Bellevue,Seattle,Spokane,Tacoma,Pasco,Olympia; Oregon, OR: Astoria, Portland, Salem, Eugene, Klamath Falls;Nevada, NV:Carson City,Ely,Tonopah,Las Vegas; California, CA: Eureka, Sacramento,Stockton,Mountain View,Berkeley,Oakland,Vacaville,San Francisco,San Jose,Monterrey,Saint Luis Obispo,Santa Barbara, Santa Monica, Pasadena, Glendale, Los Angeles, San Bernardino, Long Beach, Sunnyvale, Mission Viejo, San Diego)

Mexico
(Baja California, BCN: Mexicali, El Rosario, Playas de Rosarito, Tecate, Ensenada, San Felipe, Tijuana, Todos Santos, Jesus Maria)

France (Clipperton Island)

Britain (Pitcairn Islands)

GMT - 7 hours

Canada
(Yukon,YT:Dawson,Whitehorse;North West Territories,NT:Yellowknife,Resolution;Alberta,AB:Peace River,Fort McMurray, Calgary,Edmonton)

America
(Montana, MT: Helena, Billings, Red Lodge, Anaconda, Livingston, Bozeman;
the west of North Dakota, ND; west South Dakota, SD, Rapid City;
the south of Idaho, ID; Wyoming, WY: Sheridan, Rock Springs, Laramie, Cheyenne; west Nebraska, NE; Utah, UT:
Ogden, Salt Lake City, Provo; Colorado, CO: Denver, Pueblo, Trinidad; Arizona, AZ: Jerome, Phoenix, Globe, Morenci,
Yuma, Tucson, Tombstone, Bisbee; New Mexico, NM: Raton, Los Alamos, Santa Fe, another Las Vegas, Albuquerque,
Socorro, Roswell, Carlsbad)

Mexico
(Baja California Sur, BCS: La Paz, Comondu, Mulege, Loreto, San Lucas, Loreto, Rosalia; Sonora, SON: Hermosillo, Obregon,
Nogales, Guaymas, Alamos, Mochis, Topolobampo; Sinoloa, SIN: Culiacan, Ahome, Mazatlan, Guasave, El Fuerte, Sinaloa;
Nayarit, NAY: Tepic, Tuxpan, Acaponeta, Compostela; after 1998 Chihuahua, CUU: Juarez, Delicias, Parral, Cuauhtemoc)

GMT - 6 hours

Canada
(a part of Nunavut, NU, from the former North West Territories: Resolute , Gjoa Haven, Rankin Inlet, Baker Lake;
Saskatchewan, SK: Saskatoon, Regina, Moose Jaw,Yorkton, Estevan, Corman Park; Manitoba, MB:Winnipeg, Port Nelson,
Churchill, Thompson, Dauphin; the north west of Ontario, ON: Sandy Lake)

America
(Minnesota, MN: Minneapolis, Saint Paul, Duluth; east North Dakota, ND: Minot, Bismarck; east South Dakota, SD:
Pierre, Sioux Falls; Wisconsin, WI: Milwaukee, Madison; Iowa, IA: Des Moines, Cedar Rapids; Nebraska, NE: Omaha,
Lincoln; Illinois, IL: Chicago, Urbana, Champaign, Springfield, Peoria; Kansas, KS: Wichita, Topeka, Galena, Hutchinson;
north west, Gary, and south west, Evansville, of Indiana, IN; Missouri, MO: Saint Louis, Springfield; west Kentucky, KY;
west Tennessee, TN: Memphis; Oklahoma, OK: Tulsa, Durant; Arkansas, AR: Little Rock, Hotsprings; Texas, TX,
Houston, Dallas, San Antonio, Waco, Amarillo, Austin, Galveston;Louisiana, LA: New Orleans, Baton Rouge, Shreveport;
Mississippi, MS: Meridian, Jackson; Alabama, AL: Huntsville, Montgomery, Mobile; north west Florida, FL: Pensacola)

Mexico
(Coahuila,CA: Saltillo, Piedras Negras; Nuevo Leon, NLE: Monterrey, Villaldalma, Galeana; Tamaulipas, TMP: Ciudad Victoria,
Matamoros, Xicotencatl; Durango,DUR: Villa Hidalgo, Inde, Rodeo, El Oro; Zacatecas, ZAC: Fresnillo, Sombrerete; San Luis Potosi,
SLP: Zaragoza, Venado, Coxcatlan, Ramos; Aguascalientes, AGS: Asientos, Romos, Tepezala; Veracruz, VER: Xalapa Enriquez,
Coatzacoalcos, Cordoba; Jalisco, JAL: Guadalajara, Ameca, La Barca, Arandas; Guanajuato, GUA: Leon, Irapuato, Saramanca;
Queretaro, QRO: Guamichi, Arroyo Seco, Toliman; Hidalgo, HGO: Pachuca de Soto, Tulancingo, Actopan, Pan; Puebla, PUE:
Teziutlan, San Martin; Tlaxcala, TLA: Apizaco, Zacatelco; Mexico, MEX: Toluca, Ecatepec, Amoloya, Tultitlan, Zumpango; Distrito
Federal, DFE: Ciudad de Mexico; Morelos, MOR: Cuernavaca, Jiutepec; Colima, COL: Armeria, Ixtlahuacan; Michoacan, MIC:
Morelia, Uruapan, Tzintzuntzan, Zamora; Guerrerro, GRO: Chilpancingo, Acapulco, Acatepec; Oaxaca, OAX: Salina Cruz, Jamiltepec;
Chiapas, CHP: Tuxtla, San Cristobal, Tapachula; Tabasco, TAB: Villahermosa, Comalcalco; Campeche, CAM: San Francisco, Calkini;
Quintana Roo, ROO: Chetumal, Cancun, Cozumel, Isla Muheres; Yucatan, YUC: Merida, Valladolid, Ticul, Muna, Motul)

Guatemala
Belize
Honduras
El Salvador
Nicaragua
Costa Rica

Ecuador (Galapagos Islands)
Chile (Easter Island)

İnglând

GMT - 5 hours	GMT - 4 hours 30'
Canada (east Nunavut, NU, from the former North West Territories: Baffin Island: Frobisher Bay, Iqaluit ; east Ontario, ON: Chibougamau, Cochrane, Timmins, Sault Sainte Marie, Sudbury, North Bay, Ottawa, Toronto, Hamilton, London, Windsor; Quebec, QC: Port Harrison, Fort Chimo, Kuujjuaq, Fort George, Senneterre, Roberval, Arvida, Sept Iles, Trois Rivieres, Montreal) **America** (Maine, ME: Cherbrooke, Bangor, Augusta, Portland; Michigan, MI: Marquette, Grand Rapids, Lansing, Detroit; Vermont, VT: Montpelier; New Hampshire, NH: Concord, Manchester; New York, NY: Rochester, Harrison, Syracuse, Albany, Buffalo; Massachusetts, MA:, Boston, Providence, Fall River, Springfield; Rhode Island, RI: Providence; Connecticut, CT: Hartford, Bridgeport; Pennsylvania, PA: Scranton, Erie, Altoona, Pittsburg; New Jersey, NJ: Newark, South Plainfield, Philadelphia, Atlantic City; center and east Indiana, IN: South Bend, Fort Wayne, Indianapolis; Ohio, OH: Cleveland, Toledo, Akron, Canton, Columbus, Dayton, Cincinnati; West Virginia, WV: Charleston, Huntington; Delaware, DE: Dover; Maryland, MD: Baltimore, Annapolis; District of Columbia: Washington DC; east Kentucky, KY: Frankfort; Virginia, VA: Richmond, Roanoke, Norfolk; east Tennessee, TN: Knoxville; North Carolina: NC: Durham, Raleigh, Charlotte, Morrisville, Wilmington; South Carolina, SC: Columbia, Charleston; Georgia, GA: Atlanta, Augusta, Macon, Savannah, Columbus; the north and the Peninsula of Florida, FL: Tallaahasse, Jacksonville, Daytona Beach, Orlando, Tampa, Saint Petersburg, West Palm Beach, Miami, Key West) Bahamas Cuba Haiti Britain (The Islands: Cayman, Turks and Caicos) Jamaica Panama Columbia Ecuador Peru Brazil (Acre, AC: Rio Branco; the extreme west of Amazonas, AM: Cruzeiro do Sul)	Venezuela (1912 - 1964 , after 2007)
	GMT - 4 hours Denmark: (the west of Greenland: Thule) **Canada** (the majority of Labrador from New Found Land, NF: Hebron, Nain, Churchill Falls, Goose Bay; the extreme east of Quebec: Tete a la Baleine, Blanc Sablon; Prince Edward Island: Charlottetown; New Brunswick, NB: Fredericton, Saint John; Cape Breton Island: Sydney; New Scotland, NS: Halifax, Cape Breton, Port Hawksbury, New Glasgow, Truro) France (Terra Nova Island: Saint Pierre et Miquelon, 1912-1980) Britain (Bermuda Islands) Dominicania Puerto Rico Aruba Antigua Rounded Barbuda Britain (Montserrat Islands) France (Guadeloupe and Martinique Islands) Anguilla Antilles Dominica Barbados St Kitts and Nevis Grenada Trinidad Tobago Venezuela (1965 - 2007) Guyana **Brazil** (Roraima, RR: Boa Vista; east of Amazonas, AM: Manaus; Rondonia, RO: Porto Velho; Mato Grosso, MT: Cuiaba; Mato Grosso do Sul, MS: Campo Grande, Corumba) Bolivia Paraguay Chile Britain (Falkland Islands; Virgin Islands: Road Town) America (Virgin Islands: Charlotte Amalie)

GMT - 3 hours 30'

Canada (south west Labrador from New Found Land, NF: Battle Harbor;Terra Nova Island: Port aux Basques, Saint John)

GMT - 3 hours	GMT	GMT + 1 hours
Denmark (mainland Greenland: Nuuk) France (Terra Nova Island: Saint Pierre et Miquelon) Suriname France (Guyana) Brazil (Amapa, AP: Macapa; east Para, PA : Obidos, Santarem, Fortlandia, Belem, Braganca; Maranhao, MA : Sao Luis, Caxias ; Piaui, PI : Teresina ; Ceara, CE : Fortaleza; Tocantis, TO : Palmas, Tocantinopolis; Rio Grande do Norte, RN: Natal; Paraiba, PB: Joao Passoa; Pernambuco, PE: Recife, Caruaru, Sertania; Alagoas, AL: Maceio; Sergipe, SE: Aracaju; Bahia, BA: Salvador, Ilheus, Juazeiro; Distrito Federal, DF: Brasilia; Goias, GO: Goiania, Anapolis, Luziania, Rio Verde; Minas Gerais, MG: Belo Horizonte, Uberaba, Betim, Varginha; Espirito Santo, ES: Vitoria, Colatina, Aracruz; Rio de Janeiro, RJ: Nova Iguacu, Niteroi, Petropolis, Volta Redonda; Sao Paulo, SP: Guarulhos, Campinas, Sao Bernardo do Campo, Santos, Osasco, Bauru; Parana, PA: Curitiba, Londrina, Maringa, Cascavel; Santa Catarina, SC: Florianopolis, Joinville, Blumenau, Brusque; Rio Grande do Sul,RS: Porto Alegre, Pelotas, Canoas, Santa Maria, Novo Hamburgo, Osorio, Bage) Argentina Uruguay	Iceland Britain Ireland Portugal Morocco Portugal (Madeira Islands) Spain (Canaries Islands) Sahrawi Mauritania Mali Senegal Burkina Faso Gambia Guinea Bissau Guinea Togo Ghana Coast of Ivory Sierra Leone Liberia Sao Tome and Principe Faeroe Islands Britain (The Islands: Ascension, St Helena, Tristan de Cunha, Gough) Norway (Bouvet Island)	Norway Sweden Latvia (1942-1943) Lithuania (1919-1940) Denmark Poland Nederland Belgium Germany France Czechia Slovakia Luxembourg Hungary Austria Switzerland Liechtenstein Andorra Monaco Italy San Marino Slovenia Croatia Serbia Bosnia Sârpsca Herzegovina Macedonia Cosovo Albania Spain Gibraltar Malta Tunisia Algeria Libya Nigeria Niger Chad Benin Cameroon Centerafrica Equatorial Guinea Belize Congo Zaire (west: Nord Ubangi, Sud Ubangi, Mongala, Tshuapa, Équateur, Bandundu, Mai Ndombe, Kwilu, Kinshasa, Congo Central, Bas Congo, Kwango) Gabon Angola Namibia
GMT - 2 hours Brasil (Fernando de Noronha, Trindade Islands, Martim Vaz) **Britain(Georgia and Southern Sandwich Islands)**		
GMT - 1 hour Denmark (eastern Greenland: Scoresbysund) Iceland (1908 – 1968) Portugal (Azores Islands) Spain (Cape Verd Islands)		
GMT - 44' (minutes) Liberia (1919 - 1972)		

GMT + 2 hours	GMT + 3 hours	GMT + 4 hours	GMT + 5 hours
Finland Estonia Latvia Lithuania Russia (Yantarny) Belarus Ukraine Danistria Basarabia Romania Bulgaria Greece Cuzei Cyprus Cyprus Turkey Syria Lebanon Jordan Israel Palestine Egypt Libya Zaire (east: Orientale, Bas Uele, Haut Uele, Ituri, Tshopo, Nord Kivu, Sud Kivu, Sankuru, Maniema, Kasaï, Kasaï Occidental, Kasaï Oriental, Lulua, Lomami, Haut Lomami, Lualaba, Tanganyka, Haut Katanga, Katanga) Rwanda Burundi Zambia Malawi Mozambique Zimbabwe Botswana Swaziland Lesotho Southafrica	Russia (Franz Josef, Novaya Zemlya Islands; Murmansk : Polyarnyy, Moncegorsk, Apatity; Karelia: Belomorsk, Medvezhyegorsk, Kondopoga, Sortavala, Petrozavodsk, Pitkyaranta; Nenetsia: Naryan Mar ; Komi : Severny, Vorkuta, Inta, Uhta, Syktyvkar; Severodvinsk, Arhangelsk, Kotias; Sankt Petersburg: Vyborg, Puskin, Tihvin; Vologda: Cherepovets, Sokol; Novgorod: Veliky, Borovichi; Pskov: Velikye Luki; Kirov; Kostroma; Yaroslavl; Ivanovo: Kineshma; Nizhny Novgorod: Arzamas; Moscova; Mari El: Yoshkar Ola; Smolensk; Kaluga; Tula; Rjazan, Kazan; Chuvash: Cheboksary; Tatarstan: Kazan, Nizhnekamsk, Bolgar, Chistopol; Saratov: Romanovka; Mordovia: Romodanovo, Saransk; Oryol: Orel; Lipetsk: Yelets; Tambov: Michurinsk; Penza; Ulyanovsk; Kursk; Voronez; Saratov: Volsk, Barakovo; Belgorod; Volgograd: Mikhaylovka ; Rostov: Taganrog, Azov; Astrahan; Kalmykia: Elista; Stavropol: Nevinnomyssk, Georgievsk; Krasnodar: Novorossiysk, Sochi, Armavir; Adygea: Maykop; Karachay Cerkessia : Abazinsky ; Kabardia Balkaria : Nalcik; Osetia Alania : Vladikavkaz; Cecenia : Groznyy; Dagestan: Makhachkala; Yantarny 1946-1991; Samara 1931-1963) Abkhazia Osetia Georgia (1931-1940, 1946-1963, 2004-2005) (other vicinities and periods) Estonia (1943-1989) Latvia (1940-1941, 1944-1989) Lithuania (1940-1989) Belarus (1941-1991) Ukraine (1941-1990) Basarabia (1940-1990) Iraq Saudi Arabia Kuwait Bahrain Qatar Yemen Sudan Eritrea Ethiopia Djibouti Somaliland	Russia (Udmurtskaya: Glazov, Igra, Votkinsk, Izevsk Agryz, Sarapul; Samara: Togliatti, Zhiguliovsk, Pokhvistnevo, Otradny, Kinel, Novo Kuybyshevsk, Neftegorsk) (other vicinities and periods) Georgia Armenia Azerbaijan Nagorno Karabah Arabia Oman Seychelles Mauritius France (The Islands: Glorioso, Tromelin, Reunion, Crozet)	Russia (Yamalo Nenets: Drovyanoy, Gyda, Nyda, Nori, Noyabirsk, Selekhard; Khantia Mansia: Serkaly, Uray, Surgut, Nizhnevartovsk; Komi: Peles, Kosa, Kudimkar; Perm Krai : Krasnovisersk, Solikamsk, Berezniki, Kizel, Gubaha, Gremjacinsk, Krasnokamsk, Chusovoy, Lysva, Perm, Vereshchagino, Ocer, Kungur, Osa, Chernushka; Sverdolvsk : Ivdel, Severouralsk, Volchansk, Karpinsk, Krasnoturyinsk, Serov, Lobva, Kachkanar, Alapayevsk, Turinsk, Tavda, Irbit, Asbest, Talitsa, Kamyshlov, Sverdlovsk, Ekaterinburg, Pervouralsk, Revda, Kamensk, Palevskoj; Celyabinsk : Kyshtym, Karabas, Zlatoust, Satka, Bakal, Miass, Kopeysk, Korkino, Yemanzhelinsky, Plast, Yuzhnouralsk, Verkhneuralsk, Magnitogorsk, Kartaly, Bredinsky; Bashkortostan: Yanaul, Neftekamsk, Birsk, Ufa, Chishmy, Tuymazy, Oktyabrsky, Davlekanovo, Uchaly, Tirlyansky, Beloretsk, Davlekanovo, Prityutovo, Krasnousolsky, Sterlitamak, Ishimbay, Salavat, Meleuz, Kumertau, Sibay, Baymak; Dalmatovo, Kugarchinsky ; Kurgan : Shadrinsk, Shumikha, Kurtamish, Makushino; Orenburg : Abdulino, Buguruslan, Buzuluk, Sorochinsky, Saraktashsky, Mednogorsk, Akbulaksky, Orsk, Yasny, Dombarovsky, Svetlinsky) (other vicinities and periods) Kazakhstan (West, Uralsk, Atyrau, Mangystau, Aktobe) Uzbekistan Tajikistan Turkmenistan Pakistan Maldives

GMT + 3 hours 30'		GMT + 4 h 30'	
Iran	Somalia Kenya Uganda Tanzania	Afghanistan	Britain (Chagos Islands) France (The Islands: Amsterdam, Saint Paul, Kerguelen) Australia(Heard and McDonald Islands)
	Comoros France (The Islands: Mayotte, Juan de Nova, Bassas da India, Europa) Madagascar South Africa (Prince Edward Islands)		

GMT + 5 hours 30'	GMT + 5 hours 40'		GMT + 5 hours 45'
China (Kunlun 1912-1980) India Sri Lanka	Nepal (until 1986)		Nepal

GMT + 6 hours	GMT + 7 hours	GMT + 8 hours	GMT + 8 hours 45'
Russia (Omsk: Tara, Kalachinsk; Tomsk; Novosibirsk: Barabinsk, Kargat, Chulym, Berdsk, Karasuk, Suzun; Altai Krai: Talmenka, Novoaltaysk, Barnaul, Biysk, Rubtsovsk; Altai: Gorno Altaysk) Kazakhstan (North; South; East; Kostanay; Pavlodar; Akmola; Astana; Karagandy; Kyzylorda; Baikonur Russia; Zhambil) Kyrgystan China (Sikiang-Tibet 1912 - 1980) Bhutan Bangladesh Sri Lanka (1996-2006)	Russia (Severnaya Zemlya Islands; Krasnoyarsk: Taymyria Dolgano-Nenetsia Yamalia Volochansk, Norilsk, Talnah, Dudinka, Evenkia Evenkysky, Cirinda, Tutoncany, Tura, Mutoray, Krasno Igarka, Eniseisk, Lesosibirsk, Krasnoyarsk, Achinsk, Poyma, Kansk, Borodino,Uyar; Kemerovo: Yaya, Anzhero, Tayga, Yurga, Promishlennaya, Polysayevo, Belovo, Guryevsk, Kiselevsk, Prokopyevsk, Mariinsk, Novokuznetsk, Topki, Mezhdurechensk, Osinniki, Tashtagol; Hakasia: Shira, Abakan, Cernogorsk, Abaza; Tuva: Kyzyl, Ak Dovurak) (other vicinities and periods) Mongolia (west: Hovd, Bayand Ulgii, Uvs)	Russia (Irkutsk: Nakanno, Zima, Bodaybo, Kirensk, Ust Kut, Tulun, Bratsk, Hilok, Angarsk, Ust Orda; Buryat; Buryatia: Ulan Ude, Turka, Romanovka, Gusinoozersk, Onokhoy) Mongolia (the majority: Zavkhan; Govi Altai; Khovsgol; Arkhangai; Bayankhongor; Bulgan; Orkhon; Ovorkhangai; Omnogovi;Selenge;Darkhan Uul; Tov; Ulan Bator; Govisumber; Dundgovi; Khentii; Dornogovi; Dornod; Sukhbaatar) China Macao (China) Hong Kong (China) Taiwan (China) Malaysia Brunei Darussalam Singapore Philippines	Australia (the towns of Eyre highway: Eucla, Madura, Madrubilla, Border Village)
			GMT + 8 hours 30' China (Changpai 1912-1980)
GMT + 6 hours 30' Australia (Cocos Islands) Myanmar	China (Kansu-Szechuan 1912-1980) Vietnam Laos Thailand Cambodia	Indonesia (The Islands: east Kalimantan: Tarakan, Samarinda, Balikpapan, Ban Jarmasin; Sulawesi: Manado, Tomini, Ujung Pandang, Makasar; Tenggara, Bali, Sumbawa, Flores, Sumba, Alor)	**GMT + 9 hours** Russia (west and center Sakha Yakutia: Ust-Olenek, Nayba, Mirny, Malykai, Yakutsk, Neryungri; Zabaykalsky : Chita, Mogocha, Bukacaca, Chernyshevsk, Sretensk, Kokuy, Krasnokamensk, Shilka, Darasun, Borzya, Zabaykalsk; Amur: Tynda, Skovorodino, Magdagachi, Shimanovsk, Svobodny, Seryshevo, Lukachek, Blagoveshchensk, Belogorsk, Progress, Arhara)
GMT + 7 hours 20' Singapore (1933-1940)	Singapore(1905-1932) Indonesia (The Islands: Sumatera: Banda, Medan, Padang, Jambi, Padembang, Telukbetung; Belitung: Mangaar; the west of Kalimantan : Pontiana; Java: Jakarta, Bogor, Bandung, Semarang, Rembang, Surabaya, Malang)	Australia (Western Australia, WA: Derby, Halls creek, Broome, Port Hedland, Marble Bar, Orislow, Carnavon, Willuna, Mullewa, Geralton, Laverton, Leonora, Kalgoorlie, Dangara, Perth, Freemantle, Bunbury, Northcliffe, Coolgardie, Haig, Norseman, Esperance)	Coson Korea Korea Japan Palau Singapore (1942 – 1945) Micronezia (Yap Islands 1901-1969) Timor Melanesia Indonesia (The Islands: Maluku: Talaud, Morotai, Halmahera: Weda, Waigeea, Misool, Seram: Ainbon, Buru; Tanimbar, Dolak, Aru; Mapia, Biak; New Guinea: West Irian, Sorony, Mapi, Marauk)
GMT + 7 hours 30' Singapore (1941- 1942, 1945 - 1982)	Australia (Christmas Island)		

GMT + 9 hours 30'
Australia (Northern Territory, NT: Darwin, Burrundie, Katherine, Birdum, Borroloola, Daly Waters, Newcastle Waters, Tennant Creek,Barrow Creek, Coniston, Alice Springs, Charlotte Waters, Engoordina; South Australia, SA: Oodnadatta, Marre, Port Augusta, Watson, Penong, Port Lincoln, Port Pirie, Adelaide, Bordertown, Kingston; Broken Hill)

GMT + 10 hours
Rusia (New Siberia Islands, central Sakha Yakutia: Kular, Verkhoyansk, Tomtor, Brindakit; Habarovsk: Ohotsk, Komsomolsk, Sahalin; Primorsky: Vladivostok, Nahodka)
Mariana Islands Guam (America) Micronezia (Chuuk, Yap Islands)
Papua New Guinea
Australia (Queensland, QLD: Somerset, Coen, Cooktown, Cairos, Normanton, Forsayth, Burketown, Lobbyre, Townsville, Mount Isa, Duchess, Dajarra, Winton, Nughenden, Longreach, Quilpie, Cunnamulla, Charleville, Rockhampton, Bundaberg, Maryborough, Toowoomba, Ipswich, Brisbane, the Coral Sea Islands; New South Wales, NSW: Bourke, Walgett, Tamworth, Dubbo, Orange, Maitland, Broken Hill, Newcastle, Cessnok, Sydney, Wollogong, Goulburn, Canberra, Bombala, Albury; Victoria, VIC: Mildura, Bendigo, Melbourne, Morvell, Orbost, Portland, Ballarat, Geelong; Tasmania, TAS: Smithton, Lauceston, Qeenstown, Hobart; Macquarie Island)

GMT + 10 hours 30'	GMT + 11 hours	GMT + 11 h 30'	GMT + 12 hours
Australia (Lord Hawe Island, during the daylight saving time are added only 30')	Russia (east Sakha Yakutia: Logaskino, Chersky, Argahtah, Nalimsk, Nelemnoe; Magadan: Susuman, Ola, Sinegorye, Garmanda, Tahtoyamsk) Micronesia (Pohnpei, Kosrae Islands) Solomon Islands Vanuatu France (New Caledonia)	Australia (Norfolk Island)	Russia (Chukotka: Pevek, Bilibino, Provideniya, Anadyr, Markovo; Kamchatka Koryaskiy: Ust Voyampolka, Ust Hayryuzovo, Apuka, Uka, Palana, Ust Kamchatsky, Petropavlovsk, Mohovaya, Elizovo) America (Wake Island) France (Wallis and Foutuna Islands) Micronezia (Kosrae Islands 1969-1999) Nauru Tuvalu Fiji Kiribati (Gilbert Islands) Marshall Islands New Zeeland
GMT + 12 h 45' New Zeeland (Chatham Islands)	GMT + 13 hours Kiribati (Phoenix Islands) Tonga		GMT + 14 hours Kiribati (Kiritimati, Line Islands)

http://en.wikipedia.org/wiki/List_of_country_names_in_various_languages
http://en.wikipedia.org/wiki/List_of_country_name_etymologies
http://en.wikipedia.org/wiki/Category:Time_zones

Time zones	For the calculation of the 8 pillars, on the vertical we see that before the <u>standard</u> hour **00** is a standard date of birth, and after is another, but for the calculi we use: www.astro.com or maps and tables by years																							
GMT-12	12	13	14	15	16	17	18	19	20	21	22	23	**00**	1	2	3	4	5	6	7	8	9	10	11
GMT-11	13	14	15	16	17	18	19	20	21	22	23	**00**	1	2	3	4	5	6	7	8	9	10	11	12
GMT-10	14	15	16	17	18	19	20	21	22	23	**00**	1	2	3	4	5	6	7	8	9	10	11	12	13
GMT-9 30'	14:30	15:30	16:30	17:30	18:30	19:30	20:30	21:30	22:30	23:30	00:30	1:30	2:30	3:30	4:30	5:30	6:30	7:30	8:30	9:30	10:30	11:30	12:30	13:30
GMT-9	15	16	17	18	19	20	21	22	23	**00**	1	2	3	4	5	6	7	8	9	10	11	12	13	14
GMT-8 30'	15:30	16:30	17:30	18:30	19:30	20:30	21:30	22:30	23:30	00:30	1:30	2:30	3:30	4:30	5:30	6:30	7:30	8:30	9:30	10:30	11:30	12:30	13:30	14:30
GMT-8	16	17	18	19	20	21	22	23	**00**	1	2	3	4	5	6	7	8	9	10	11	12	13	14	15
GMT-7	17	18	19	20	21	22	23	**00**	1	2	3	4	5	6	7	8	9	10	11	12	13	14	15	16
GMT-6	18	19	20	21	22	23	**00**	1	2	3	4	5	6	7	8	9	10	11	12	13	14	15	16	17
GMT-5	19	20	21	22	23	**00**	1	2	3	4	5	6	7	8	9	10	11	12	13	14	15	16	17	18
GMT-4	20	21	22	23	**00**	1	2	3	4	5	6	7	8	9	10	11	12	13	14	15	16	17	18	19
GMT-3 30'	20:30	21:30	22:30	23:30	00:30	1:30	2:30	3:30	4:30	5:30	6:30	7:30	8:30	9:30	10:30	11:30	12:30	13:30	14:30	15:30	16:30	17:30	18:30	19:30
GMT-3	21	22	23	**00**	1	2	3	4	5	6	7	8	9	10	11	12	13	14	15	16	17	18	19	20
GMT-2	22	23	**00**	1	2	3	4	5	6	7	8	9	10	11	12	13	14	15	16	17	18	19	20	21
GMT-1	23	**00**	1	2	3	4	5	6	7	8	9	10	11	12	13	14	15	16	17	18	19	20	21	22
GMT-44'	23:16	00:16	1:16	2:16	3:16	4:16	5:16	6:16	7:16	8:16	9:16	10:16	11:16	12:16	13:16	14:16	15:16	16:16	17:16	18:16	19:16	20:16	21:16	22:16
GMT	**00**	1	2	3	4	5	6	7	8	9	10	11	12	13	14	15	16	17	18	19	20	21	22	23
GMT+1	1	2	3	4	5	6	7	8	9	10	11	12	13	14	15	16	17	18	19	20	21	22	23	**00**
GMT+2	2	3	4	5	6	7	8	9	10	11	12	13	14	15	16	17	18	19	20	21	22	23	**00**	1
GMT+3	3	4	5	6	7	8	9	10	11	12	13	14	15	16	17	18	19	20	21	22	23	**00**	1	2
GMT+3 30'	3:30	4:30	5:30	6:30	7:30	8:30	9:30	10:30	11:30	12:30	13:30	14:30	15:30	16:30	17:30	18:30	19:30	20:30	21:30	22:30	23:30	00:30	1:30	2:30
GMT+4	4	5	6	7	8	9	10	11	12	13	14	15	16	17	18	19	20	21	22	23	**00**	1	2	3
GMT+4 30'	4:30	5:30	6:30	7:30	8:30	9:30	10:30	11:30	12:30	13:30	14:30	15:30	16:30	17:30	18:30	19:30	20:30	21:30	22:30	23:30	00:30	1:30	2:30	3:30
GMT+5	5	6	7	8	9	10	11	12	13	14	15	16	17	18	19	20	21	22	23	**00**	1	2	3	4
GMT+5 30'	5:30	6:30	7:30	8:30	9:30	10:30	11:30	12:30	13:30	14:30	15:30	16:30	17:30	18:30	19:30	20:30	21:30	22:30	23:30	00:30	1:30	2:30	3:30	4:30
GMT+5 40'	5:40	6:40	7:40	8:40	9:40	10:40	11:40	12:40	13:40	14:40	15:40	16:40	17:40	18:40	19:40	20:40	21:40	22:40	23:40	00:40	1:40	2:40	3:40	4:40
GMT+5 45'	5:45	6:45	7:45	8:45	9:45	10:45	11:45	12:45	13:45	14:45	15:45	16:45	17:45	18:45	19:45	20:45	21:45	22:45	23:45	00:45	1:45	2:45	3:45	4:45
GMT+6	6	7	8	9	10	11	12	13	14	15	16	17	18	19	20	21	22	23	**00**	1	2	3	4	5
GMT+6 30'	6:30	7:30	8:30	9:30	10:30	11:30	12:30	13:30	14:30	15:30	16:30	17:30	18:30	19:30	20:30	21:30	22:30	23:30	00:30	1:30	2:30	3:30	4:30	5:30
GMT+7	7	8	9	10	11	12	13	14	15	16	17	18	19	20	21	22	23	**00**	1	2	3	4	5	6
GMT+7 20'	7:20	8:20	9:20	10:20	11:20	12:20	13:20	14:20	15:20	16:20	17:20	18:20	19:20	20:20	21:20	22:20	23:20	00:20	1:20	2:20	3:20	4:20	5:20	6:20
GMT+7 30'	7:30	8:30	9:30	10:30	11:30	12:30	13:30	14:30	15:30	16:30	17:30	18:30	19:30	20:30	21:30	22:30	23:30	00:30	1:30	2:30	3:30	4:30	5:30	6:30
GMT+8 Beijing	8	9	10	11	12	13	14	15	16	17	18	19	20	21	22	23	**00**	1	2	3	4	5	6	7
GMT+8 30'	8:30	9:30	10:30	11:30	12:30	13:30	14:30	15:30	16:30	17:30	18:30	19:30	20:30	21:30	22:30	23:30	00:30	1:30	2:30	3:30	4:30	5:30	6:30	7:30
GMT+8 45'	8:45	9:45	10:45	11:45	12:45	13:45	14:45	15:45	16:45	17:45	18:45	19:45	20:45	21:45	22:45	23:45	00:45	1:45	2:45	3:45	4:45	5:45	6:45	7:45
GMT+9	9	10	11	12	13	14	15	16	17	18	19	20	21	22	23	**00**	1	2	3	4	5	6	7	8
GMT+9 30'	9:30	10:30	11:30	12:30	13:30	14:30	15:30	16:30	17:30	18:30	19:30	20:30	21:30	22:30	23:30	00:30	1:30	2:30	3:30	4:30	5:30	6:30	7:30	8:30
GMT+10	10	11	12	13	14	15	16	17	18	19	20	21	22	23	**00**	1	2	3	4	5	6	7	8	9
GMT+10 30'	10:30	11:30	12:30	13:30	14:30	15:30	16:30	17:30	18:30	19:30	20:30	21:30	22:30	23:30	00:30	1:30	2:30	3:30	4:30	5:30	6:30	7:30	8:30	9:30
GMT+11	11	12	13	14	15	16	17	18	19	20	21	22	23	**00**	1	2	3	4	5	6	7	8	9	10
GMT+11 30'	11:30	12:30	13:30	14:30	15:30	16:30	17:30	18:30	19:30	20:30	21:30	22:30	23:30	00:30	1:30	2:30	3:30	4:30	5:30	6:30	7:30	8:30	9:30	10:30
GMT+12	12	13	14	15	16	17	18	19	20	21	22	23	**00**	1	2	3	4	5	6	7	8	9	10	11
GMT+12 45'	12:45	13:45	14:45	15:45	16:45	17:45	18:45	19:45	20:45	21:45	22:45	23:45	00:45	1:45	2:45	3:45	4:45	5:45	6:45	7:45	8:45	9:45	10:45	11:45
GMT+13	13	14	15	16	17	18	19	20	21	22	23	**00**	1	2	3	4	5	6	7	8	9	10	11	12
GMT+14	14	15	16	17	18	19	20	21	22	23	**00**	1	2	3	4	5	6	7	8	9	10	11	12	13

www.wikipedia.org/wiki/List_of_time_zones

www.wikipedia.org/wiki/Category:Hemispheres www.wikipedia.org/wiki/Category:Holidays

www.wikipedia.org/wiki/Category:Seasons www.wikipedia.org/wiki/Category:Saints

The calculation of all the Chinese pillars:

The previous examples are valid only if it wasn't the daylight saving time. With the three components: the place, the official date (from the identification documents) and the official hour of birth (from the register of the hospital of birth), we can find the existence of the daylight saving time, so correct calculi with the standard time found.

Finding the daylight saving time and the differences of time zone:

The daylight saving time can be found very exactly at the next internet address for the classical zodiac:

www.astro.com (by introducing at chart and my astro the official date and hour, so the date from the identification card and the hour from the births register, we find in detail everything for any town and any time); at:

www.timezoneconverter.com or at

www.timeanddate.com

During the calculi of a date and hour of birth, when we see daylight saving time, that means it was the summer time, and if we see standard time that means it was the winter time.

Consequently we find that it was the daylight saving time.

In order to find how much it lasts, we calculate for a date (for example July for the southern hemisphere and January for the northern hemisphere) and the same official hour from the winter that was before the date of birth, the standard time, by subtracting from the daylight saving time the standard time, obtaining the minutes(rarely), an hour(most frequently) or the summer hours(rarely). Let's not forget that when it is winter in the southern hemisphere of the Earth, in the northern one it is summer, so also the eventual daylight saving time is opposed in calendar for the two hemispheres.

We obtain **the 4 pillars from the place of birth** by subtracting from the official date and hour of birth, the daylight saving time.

To find **the 4 pillars from Beijing**, we use the chart where we introduced the official hour from that locality(the summer or winter hour), written here, time, we observe what was the GMT(written here Universal Time,UT) and we add to this: 8 hours.

Therefore it is possible the entire official date and hour of birth to change.

Explanations of the hours are at the classical zodiac chapter.

The example 1:

To calculate the Chinese pillars we must use www.astro.com like that:

- we choose chart and there we introduce the asked dates like the place, the date (from the identity card) and the official hour of birth(from the births' register): Melbourne, I 1 2006, 00:30, during the calculi it is showed if the daylight saving time existed,in this case it exists and we see that we are 11 hours from the GMT meridian

- then we take a date from the local winter, that precedes the birth date, and the same official hour, lets say VII 2 2005, 00:30, Melbourne, we see that it was the standard time and that we are 10 hours from the GMT meridian

So it was 1 daylight saving time hour.

- by subtracting the daylight saving time hour we obtain the standard date and hour: XII 31 2005,23:30, with those figures calculating the pillars from the place of birth

- we add 8 hours to the GMT date and time XII 31 2005,13:30 and we obtain the standard date and hour from Beijing: XII 31 2005,21:30, with these ciphers calculating the pillars from Beijing

The place, date and hour of birth	Chinese year	Chinese month	Chinese day	Chinese hour	The 8 Chinese pillars
1) official time:Melbourne, Australia I 1 2006, 00:30					
standard time: Melbourne, Australia XII 31 2005, 23:30	rooster t	rat E	buffalo e	rat F	the 4 pillars from the place of birth
st. Beijing,Shanghai time: China XII 31 2005, 21:30	rooster t	rat E	buffalo e	pig t	the 4 pillars from Pechin, Pekin, Peking, Peiching, Pequim, Peiping, Beiping, Beijing
2) official time: Sapporo, Japan II 4 2006, 00:30					
standard time: Sapporo, Japan II 4 2006, 00:30	dog F	tiger M	rat T	rat T	the 4 pillars from the place of birth
st. Beijing,Shanghai time: China II 3 2006, 23:30	rooster t	buffalo e	pig w	rat T	the 4 pillars from Pechin, Pekin, Peking, Peiching, Pequim, Peiping, Beiping, Beijing
3) official time:Honolulu, America IV 4 2006, 10:40					
standard time: Honolulu America IV 4 2006, 10:40	dog F	rabbit m	pig w	snake f	the 4 pillars from the place of birth
st. Beijing,Shanghai time: China IV 5 2006, 4:40	dog F	dragon W	rat T	tiger F	the 4 pillars from Pechin, Pekin, Peking, Peiching, Pequim, Peiping, Beiping, Beijing
4) official time: New York, America VI 5 2006, 22:50					
standard time: New York, America VI 5 2006, 21:50	dog F	snake w	buffalo t	pig f	the 4 pillars from the place of birth
st. Beijing,Shanghai time: China VI 6 2006, 10:50	dog F	horse T	tiger F	snake w	the 4 pillars from Pechin, Pekin, Peking, Peiching, Pequim, Peiping, Beiping, Beijing
5) official time: Ottawa, Canada VI 5 2006, 19:50					
standard time: Ottawa, Canada VI 5 2006, 18:50	dog F	snake w	buffalo t	rooster t	the 4 pillars from the place of birth
st. Beijing,Shanghai time: China VI 6 2006, 8:50	dog F	horse T	tiger F	dragon W	the 4 pillars from Pechin, Pekin, Peking, Peiching, Pequim, Peiping, Beiping, Beijing
6) official time:Sighetul Marmației, Romania VI 5 2006, 19:50					
standard time: Sighetul Marmației, Romania VI 5 2006, 18:50	dog F	snake a	buffalo t	rooster t	the 4 pillars from the place of birth
st. Beijing,Shanghai time: China VI 6 2006, 12:50	dog F	horse T	tiger F	horse T	the 4 pillars from Pechin, Pekin, Peking, Peiching, Pequim, Peiping, Beiping, Beijing

Discussions:

Three persons born at the same distance from each other and at the same time, two of these being born in a time zone at 100 m from each other, and the third one in another time zone, but also at 100 m from the first two (those who live at the border between two time zones), can have different Chinese signs. The only explanation would be given by the esoteric importance of the time conventions.

The base of all the zodiacal compatibilities:

For an ideal zodiacal compatibility we find the ideal of each pillar (year, month, day, hour) and thus we obtain the ideal Chinese birth dates (at the end of the book there is a concrete example):

Binomial	Maximized monachism	Minimized monachism	Maximized familism	Minimized familism
1 rat T	dragon W dragon F monkey W monkey F	horse M horse E horses animals of M or E	buffalo e	sheep m sheep animals of m
2 buffalo t	snake w snake f rooster w rooster f	sheep m sheep e sheep animals of m or e	rat M	horse E horses animals of E
3 tiger F	horse T horse E dog T dog E	monkey W monkey M monkeys animals of W or M	pig m	snake w snakes animals of w
4 rabbit f	sheep t sheep e pig t pig e	rooster w rooster m roosters animals of w or m	dog W	dragon M dragons animals of M
5 dragon E	rat F rat M monkey F monkey M	dog T dog W dogs animals of T or W	rooster w	rabbit t rabbits animals of t
6 snake e	buffalo f buffalo m rooster f rooster m	pig t pig w pigs animals of t or w	monkey T	tiger W tigers animals of W
7 horse M	tiger E tiger W dog E dog W	rat F rat T rats animals of F or T	sheep t	buffalo f buffalos animals of f
8 sheep m	rabbit e rabbit w pig e pig w	buffalo f buffalo t buffalos animals of f or t	horse F	rat T rats animals of T
9 monkey W	rat M rat T dragon M dragon T	tiger E tiger F tigers animals of E or F	snake f	pig e pigs animals of e
10 rooster w	buffalo m buffalo t snake m snake t	rabbit e rabbit f rabbits animals of e or f	dragon E	dog F dogs animals of F
11 dog T	tiger W tiger F horse W horse F	dragon M dragon E dragons animals of M or E	rabbit e	rooster m roosters animals of m
12 pig t	rabbit w rabbit f sheep w sheep f	snake m snake e snakes animals of m or e	tiger M	monkey E monkeys animals of E

Binomial	Maximized monachism	Minimized monachism	Maximized familism	Minimized familism
13 rat F	dragon T dragon E monkey T monkey E	horse W horse M horses animals of W or M	buffalo m	sheep w sheep animals of w
14 buffalo f	snake t snake e rooster t rooster e	sheep w sheep m sheep animals of w or m	rat W	horse M horses animals of M
15 tiger E	horse F horse M dog F dog M	monkey T monkey W monkeys animals of T or W	pig w	snake t snakes animals of t
16 rabbit e	sheep f sheep m pig f pig m	rooster t rooster w roosters animals of t or w	dog T	dragon W dragons animals of W
17 dragon M	rat E rat W monkey E monkey W	dog F dog T dogs animals of F or T	rooster t	rabbit f rabbits animals of f
18 snake m	buffalo e buffalo w rooster e rooster w	pig f pig t pigs animals of f or t	monkey F	tiger T tigers animals of T
19 horse W	tiger M tiger T dog M dog T	rat E rat F rats animals of E or F	sheep f	buffalo e buffalos animals of e
20 sheep w	rabbit m rabbit t pig m pig t	buffalo e buffalo f buffalos animals of e or f	horse E	rat F rats animals of F
21 monkey T	rat W rat F dragon W dragon F	tiger M tiger P tigers animals of M or P	snake p	pig m pigs animals of m
22 rooster t	buffalo w buffalo f snake w snake f	rabbit m rabbit e rabbits animals of m or e	dragon M	dog E dogs animals of E
23 dog F	tiger T tiger E horse T horse E	dragon W dragon M dragons animals of W or M	rabbit m	rooster w roosters animals of w
24 pig f	rabbit t rabbit e sheep t sheep e	snake w snake m snakes animals of w or m	tiger W	monkey M monkeys animals of M

Binomial	Maximized monachism	Minimized monachism	Maximized familism	Minimized familism
25 rat E	dragon F dragon M monkey F monkey M	horse T horse W horses animals of T or W	buffalo w	sheep t sheep animals of t
26 buffalo e	snake f snake m rooster f rooster m	sheep t sheep w sheep animals of t or w	rat T	horse W horses animals of W
27 tiger M	horse E horse W dog E dog W	monkey F monkey T monkeys animals of F or T	pig t	snake f snakes animals of f
28 rabbit m	sheep e sheep w pig e pig w	rooster f rooster t roosters animals of f or t	dog F	dragon T dragons animals of T
29 dragon W	rat M rat T monkey M monkey T	dog E dog F dogs animals of E or F	rooster f	rabbit e rabbits animals of e
30 snake w	buffalo m buffalo t rooster m rooster t	pig e pig f pigs animals of e or f	monkey E	tiger F tigers animals of F
31 horse T	tiger W tiger F dog W dog F	rat M rat E rats animals of M or E	sheep e	buffalo m buffalos animals of m
32 sheep t	rabbit w rabbit f pig w pig f	buffalo m buffalo e buffalos animals of m or e	horse M	rat E rats animals of E
33 monkey F	rat T rat E dragon T dragon E	tiger W tiger M tigers animals of W or M	snake m	pig w pigs animals of w
34 rooster f	buffalo t buffalo e snake t snake e	rabbit w rabbit m rabbits animals of w or m	dragon W	dog M dogs animals of M
35 dog E	tiger F tiger M horse F horse M	dragon T dragon W dragons animals of T or W	rabbit w	rooster t roosters animals of t
36 pig e	rabbit f rabbit m sheep f sheep m	snake t snake w snakes animals of t or w	tiger T	monkey W monkeys animals of W

Binomial	Maximized monachism	Minimized monachism	Maximized familism	Minimized familism
37 rat M	dragon E dragon W monkey E monkey W	horse F horse T horses animals of F or T	buffalo t	sheep f sheep animals of f
38 buffalo m	snake e snake w rooster e rooster w	sheep f sheep t sheep animals of f or t	rat F	horse T horses animals of T
39 tiger W	horse M horse T dog M dog T	monkey E monkey F monkeys animals of E or F	pig f	snake e snakes animals of e
40 rabbit w	sheep m sheep t pig m pig t	rooster e rooster f roosters animals of e or f	dog E	dragon F dragons animals of F
41 dragon T	rat W rat F monkey W monkey F	dog M dog E dogs animals of M or E	rooster e	rabbit m rabbits animals of m
42 snake t	buffalo w buffalo f rooster w rooster f	pig m pig e pigs animals of m or e	monkey M	tiger E tigers animals of E
43 horse F	tiger T tiger E dog T dog E	rat W rat M rats animals of W or M	sheep m	buffalo w buffalos animals of w
44 sheep f	rabbit t rabbit e pig t pig e	buffalo w buffalo m buffalos animals of w or m	horse W	rat M rats animals of M
45 monkey E	rat F rat M dragon F dragon M	tiger T tiger W tigers animals of T or W	snake w	pig t pigs animals of t
46 rooster e	buffalo f buffalo m snake f snake m	rabbit t rabbit w rabbits animals of t or w	dragon T	dog W dogs animals of W
47 dog M	tiger E tiger W horse E horse W	dragon F dragon T dragons animals of F or T	rabbit t	rooster f roosters animals of f
48 pig m	rabbit e rabbit w sheep e sheep w	snake f snake t snakes animals of f or t	tiger F	monkey T monkeys animals of T

Binomial	Maximized monachism	Minimized monachism	Maximized familism	Minimized familism
49 rat W	dragon M dragon T monkey M monkey T	horse E horse F horses animals of E or F	buffalo f	sheep e sheep animals of e
50 buffalo w	snake m snake t rooster m rooster t	sheep e sheep f sheep animals of e or f	rat E	horse F horses animals of F
51 tiger T	horse W horse F dog W dog F	monkey M monkey E monkeys animals of M or E	pig e	snake m snakes animals of m
52 rabbit t	sheep w sheep f pig w pig f	rooster m rooster e roosters animals of m or e	dog M	dragon E dragons animals of E
53 dragon F	rat T rat E monkey T monkey E	dog W dog M dogs animals of W or M	rooster m	rabbit w rabbits animals of w
54 snake f	buffalo t buffalo e rooster t rooster e	pig w pig m pigs animals of w or m	monkey W	tiger M tigers animals of M
55 horse E	tiger F tiger M dog F dog M	rat T rat W rats animals of T or W	sheep w	buffalo t buffalos animals of t
56 sheep e	rabbit f rabbit m pig f pig m	buffalo t buffalo w buffalos animals of t or w	horse T	rat W rats animals of W
57 monkey M	rat E rat W dragon E dragon W	tiger F tiger T tigers animals of F or T	snake t	pig f pigs animals of f
58 rooster m	buffalo e buffalo w snake e snake w	rabbit f rabbit t rabbits animals of f or t	dragon F	dog T dogs animals of T
59 dog W	tiger M tiger T horse M horse T	dragon F dragon E dragons animals of F or E	rabbit f	rooster e roosters animals of e
60 pig w	rabbit m rabbit t sheep m sheep t	snake f snake e snakes animals of f or e	tiger E	monkey F monkeys animals of F

The Chinese day from the place of birth (if it was the daylight saving time, some examples can be also from the anterior Chinese day from the place of birth):

The day of the rat:

Adam Charles Clayton-bass,U2(M),Steven Adler-drums,Hollywood Roses(T),Vilius Alesius-voice,Skamp(M),Alfonso-RBD(E),Gem Colin Murray Archer–guitar,Oasis (M),Dana Ashbrook-Bobby Robert,Twin Peaks(E),Paul Baran(E),Omar Hasan Ahmad Al Bashir(T),Max Beasley-Charlie,Hotel Babylon(M),Victoria Caroline Adams Beckham Posh–Spice Girls(E),Maria Bello-Anna,ER(W),Sali Ram Berisha(W),Christopher George Latore Wallace Notorious BIG(W),Abdelaziz Bouteflika(E),Marlon Brando(W),Warren Buffett(W),Sandra Bullock(F),Diosdado Cabello Rondon(E),Felipe de Jesus Calderon Hinojosa(E),Rafael Francisco Alburquerque De Castro(E),Ray Charles Robinson(F), Arlindo Chinaglia(E),Claudia Pătrăşcanu-Exotic(W),Maurice Colbourne–Tom,Howards' Way(T),Robbie Coltrane-Hagrid,Harry Potter(T),Pascal Couchepin(E),Denise Crosby-Tasha,Star Trek(M),Kemal Derviş(M),Dustin Diamond-Screech,Saved by the Bell(T), Mohamed Dileita(E),Theodore Dreiser(M),Gloria Estefan(T),Linda Evangelista(T),Frida-ABBA(E),Calista Flockhart-Ally McBeal(T),Don Franklin-Jonathan Ford,SeaQuest(F), Jennie Garth-Kelly,Beverly Hills(T),Laurent Koudou Gbagbo(M),Virgil Hamlin Good Junior(T),Maggie Grace-Shannon,Lost(W),Hugh Grant(M),Brian Austin Green-David Silver,Beverly Hills(W),Greiere-drums,AnimalX(F),Menachem Hacohen–rabbi(E), Alyson Hannigan-Michelle,American Pie(T),Salma Hayek(T),Victor Hănescu-tennis (M),John Winston Howard(T),Ştefan Hruşcă(W),Ion Iliescu(W),Amy Irving(T),Julia Chelaru-Exotic(T),Mary Kate MK and Asley-Full House(E),Malcolm David Kelley-Walt,Lost(E),Kathleen Kinmont(E),James Knobeloch–Jake,Dr. Quinn(W),Ashton Kutcher(M),Christopher Lambert(M),Joe Lando-Sully,Dr. Quinn(F),Avril Lavigne(T), Sergei Nikolaevich Lebedev(T),Tim Timothy John Berners Lee(M),J Lo Jennifer Lynn Lopez(M),Latoya Luckett-Destiny's Child(E),Alhaji Aliu Mahama(F),John Paul Manley (M),Handke Giussepe Gino Manzotti-DJ Project(W),Jean Marais(F),Khaled Mardam Bey(E),Hattie McDaniel–Mammy,Gone with the Wind(E),George Stanley McGovern (E),Jim Morrison-The Doors(M),Nick-Backstreet Boys(M),Nico Matei(W),Robert Kuok Hock Nien(W),Chuck Norris(W),Oana–Activ(E),Malia Ann Obama(W),Devisingh Patil-president(T),Franka Potente(T),Dan Piţa(F),Dumitru Prunariu-astronaut(F),Ahmed Ali Abu Alaa Mohammed Qurei Quareia(W),Nebojsa Radmanovic(T),Alois Philipp Maria Rietberg-reigning prince(W),Lee Ryan-Blue(F),Saki(E),Carlos Santana(M),Albert Pintat Santolaria(W),Robert John Sawers(E),Seann William Scott–Stifler,American Pie (E),William Alan Shatner–James Tiberius Kirk,Star Trek(F),Michiko Shoda Showa-empress(T),Karina Medforth Mills Hohenzollern Sigmaringen-majesty(T),Alex Somers-drums,The Doo Doo Heads(M),Sorana Darclee Mohamad-ASIA(M),Tori Spelling-Donna,Beverly Hills,90210(W),Dimitrievich Sergey Stanishev(T),Jurgen Steinmetz-bass,Silent Force(W),Brenda Strong-Mary Alice,Desperate Housewives(W),Pavle Gojko Stojcevic-patriarch(M),Izzy Strandlin-guitar,Hollywood Roses(F),Gabriela Szabo(T),Ice T(T),Tedder(T),Sandrine Testude(T),Hashim Thaci(T),Antoine Albert Thibaudet(E), Tiffany Amber Thiesen(T),Charlene Tilton-Lucy,Dallas(W),Alexandru Todea-cardinal (W),Shawn Toovey-Brian,Dr. Quinn(E),Travis Landon Barker-Blink 182(T),Sid Turntables-Pyg System(F),Francisc Vaştag(M),André Armand Vingt Trois-cardinal(T), Dylan Charles Walsh(T),Julie Walters(E),Jigme Khesar Namgyel Wangchuck-dragon king(T),Maria Teresa Mestre Bourbon Parma Nassau Weilburg-grand duchess(E),Henry Charles Albert David Wales Windsor–majesty(W),John Jozef Paul Karol Wojtyla-pope (F),Virginia Woolf(T),Stephen Yardley-Ken,Howards' Way(F),Roman-Zdob şi Zdub(W)

The day of the buffalo:

Mahmoud Mazen Abu Abbas(m),Christina Maria Aguilera(t),Chad Allen-Mathew,Dr. Quinn(f),Anca Neacşu–ASIA(e),Anca Roxana Sârbu–ASIA(e),Frank Josaia Voreqe Bainimarama(w),Lee Myung Bak(m),Jean Alingué Bawoyeu(f),Marco Mark Anthony(e), Andrus Ansip(m),Charles Aznavour(m),Jose Manuel Barosso(e),Dean Olliver Barrow (m),George Bastl(f),Burton Christopher Bell-voice,Arkaea(t),Kate Blanchett(e),Sergey Brin(e),Chris Brown(t),Dragoş Vlad Caddy-BUG Mafia(t),Raul Castro(e),50 CENT Curtis James Jackson(w),Richard Chamberlain(m),Ricardo Chavira-Carlos,Desperate Housewives(e),Joan Chen-Josie,Twin Peaks(e),Melanie Jayne Chisholm Mel C–Spice Girls(w),William Jefferson Blythe Bill Clinton(t),Joan Henrietta Collins(e),Jacques Diouf (t),Michael Dorn-Worf,Star Trek(e),Eliza Dushku(f),Roy Emerson(e),Cristian Cristi Enache-voice,Direcţia 5(f),Recep Tayyip Erdogan(w),Evanescence Amy Hartzler Lynn Lee(t),Peter Falk-Columbo(w),Aretha Franklin(f),Margrethe Alexandrine Glucksburg-queen(e),Henrik Henri Marie Jean André de Laborde de Monpezat Glucksburg-majesty (w),Louis Sylvain Goma(f),Olga Gorcinschii-Millenium(w),Mark Paul Gosselaar-Zack Morris,Saved by the Bell(t),Paola Margherita Maria Antonia Consiglia Ruffo di Calabria Marie Saxe Coburg Gotha-queen(m),Kay Rala Xanana Jose Alexandre Gusmao(t),Luke Halpin-Sandy Ricks,Flipper(w),Natasha Maria Hamilton(m),Tom Thomas Jeffrey Hanks(f),Daryl Hannah(t),Terence Mario Girotti Hill(t),Alfred Hitchcock(w),Ilie Ilaşcu (f),Jean Jan Engelaar-DJ(f),Kimberly Kym Karath-Gretl,The Sound of Music(w),David E Kelley-director,Ally McBeal,Chicago Hope(m),Jackson DeForest Kelley-Leonard,Star Trek(f),Seyyed Ali Khamenei(f),Alex Kingston-Elizabeth Corday,ER(w),Cristina Elisabet Fernandez de Kirchner(m),Eduard Dzhabeyevich Kokoity(w),Demi Demetria Gene Guynes Moore Kutcher(w),Audrey Lenders-Afton Cooper,Dallas(m),Eugene Levy (t),Ieronymos Ioannis Liapis-sanctity(m),J C R Joseph Carl Robnett Licklider(m),Cirroc Lofton–Jake Sisko,Star Trek(m),Glynn Lunney(w),Ralph George Macchio(m),Shirley MacLaine(t),Mohammed bin Rashid Al Maktoum-sheikh(w),Madonna Veronica Louise Ritchie Ciccone(t),Teodoro Obiang Nguema Mbasogo(e),Leigh McCloskey-Mitch Cooper,Dallas(w),Butterfly McQueen-Prissy,Gone with the Wind(f), Janet McTeer(m), Florin Mergea(t),Nicolas Michel(m),Elaine Miles-Marilyn Whirlwind,Northern Exposure(t),Najib Mikati(e),Pervez Musharraf(m),Naledge-Kidz in the Hall(m), Edward Norton(t),Sinéad O'Connor-sanctity(m),Michelle LaVaughn Robinson Obama(t),Tamzin Outhwaite–Rebecca Mitchell,Hotel Babylon(e),Frank Oz(e),Ovidio Manuel Barbosa Pequeno(t),Alan Gabriel Ludwig Garcia Perez(w),Ellen Pompeo–Meredith,Grey's Anatomy(e),Lisa Marie Presley(m),Aisamul Haq Qureshi(e),Aishwarya Rai(m),Raluca-Bambi(m), Anders Fogh Rasmussen(f),Robert Redford(f),Mircea Rednic(f),Branscombe Richmond(m),Diana Ernestine Ross(e),Qaboos bin Said Taimur Al Bu Saidi-sultan(t), Larry Sellers–Cloud Dancing,Dr. Quinn(t),Ahmed Abdallah Mohamed Sambi(w),Putra Sampoerna(t),Marco Sanchez–Miguel,SeaQuest(e),Nicolas Paul Stéphane de Nagy Bocsa Sarkozy-president coprince(e),Doug Savant-Tom,Desperate Housewives(m),Svetlana Yevgenyevna Savitskaya(t),Claudia Schiffer(f),Komal Rajya Rana Laxmi Devi Shah-queen(e),Tuanku Nur Zahirah Shah-sultana(f),Omar Shariff(m),Sadhana Shivdasani(w), Norodom Sihamoni Sihanouk-king(t),Frank Sinatra(f),Marina Sirtis–Deanna Troi,Star Trek(e),Sissy Spacek(f),Aaron Spelling(t),Mehmet Ali Talat(w),Chen Jianghe Sukanto Tanoto(e),Muhammad Tantawy-imam(m),Paul Thomas-Finch,American Pie(f),Laszlo Tokes-sanctity(f),Ahmed Sékou Touré(f),George Siaosi Taufaahau Manumataongo Tukuaho Tupou-king(e),Alin Demeter Uzzi-BUG Mafia(f),Lark Voorhies-Lisa,Saved by the Bell(t),Danny Daniel William Wood–New Kids on the Block(e),John Watts Young (f),Jay Z(w)Asif Ali Zardari(e),Robert Bruce Zoellick(f),Preity Zinta(f),Émile Zola(m)

The day of the tiger:

Ben Affleck(E),Mahmoud Saborjhian Ahmadinejad(E),Albano Carrisi(E),Madeleine Korbelova Albright(W),Roberta Alma Anastase(E),Bocelli(W),Boniface Alexandre(T), Madchen Amick–Shelly,Twin Peaks(F),Amina Annabi(W),Christina Appelgate-Kelly,Married with Children(T),Claudia Blum de Barberi(F),Brigitte Bardot(W),Ellen Barkin(W),Bartholomew-ecumenical patriarch(W),Andreea Bănică Mitrea-Blondy(T), Boris Becker(M),Stephanie Beecham–Kristin,SeaQuest(E),Marek Belka(T),Silvio Berlusconi(T),Dan Bitman-Holograf(F),Bouasone Bouphavanh(M),Peter Burian(W), Linda Cardellini–Samantha,ER(W),Rodrigo Borja Cevallos(F),Christodoulos-sanctity (T),Patrice Clerc(W),Hillary Diane Rodham Clinton(E),Chris Columbus-director,Harry Potter(M),John Corbett-Chris,Northern Exposure(W),Corey-voice,Pyg System(E),Tom Thomas Mapother Cruise(W),Anthony Daniels-C3P0 robot,Star(F),Bette Davis(M), Cristina Deleanu(W),Rodrigo Malmierca Diaz(T),Snoop Dogg(T),Hector Elizondo-Dr. Phillip Watters,Chicago Hope(E),Estelle Fanta Swaray(M),Garibaldi Alves Filho(T), Dexter Fletcher(M),Andrew Fletcher-bass,Depeche Mode(W),Jodie Foster(M), Galsworthy(F),Ava Gardner(F),Jennifer Garner(E),Boy George(E),Whoopi Goldberg(E), Albert Grimaldi-serene majesty sovereign prince(M),Alfred Gusenbauer(F),Geir Hilmar Haarde (E),Katherine Heigl(M),James Hetfield-Metallica(E),Edward Highmore–Leo, Howards' Way(F),Cypress Hill(E),Robert Murray Hill(W),Jose Manuel Ramos Horta (M),Howie Howard Dwaine Dorough Flores-Backstreet Boys(M),William Hurt(T), Clifford Straughn Husbands(F),Enrique Iglesias(T),Kim Yong Il(F),Frederick Reginald Michael Ironside–Oliver,SeaQuest(E),Doru Isăroiu(T),Michael-Jacksons(E),Erika Jennings-Skamp(M),Joey-drums,Pyg System(W),Julia-TATU(M),Kafelnikov(M),Cody Kasch(W),Nashawn Kearse(F),Aqeel Khan(W),Jane Krakowski–Elaine,Ally McBeal (W),Vivien Mary Hartley Olivier Leigh(M),Evangeline Lilly-Kate,Lost(W),Annette Lu (W),George Lucas-director,Star(E),Mack10(F),Jean Marais(F),Ismael Abraao Gaspar Martins(T),Steve Dick Tennyson Matenje(T),Thabo Mbeki(W),Paul McCartney-The Beatles(W),Frances McDormand(F),Dannii Danielle Jane Minogue(E),Frederic Mistral (E),Keith Claudius Mitchell(M),Maxwell Mkwezalamba(E),Ovidiu Iuliu Moldovan(W), Alicia Moore-voice,Pink(E),Wanya Jermaine Morris-Boyz II Men(F),Lucian Mureşan-sanctity(E),Eddie Regan Murphy(F),Rafael Nadal(E),Giorgio Napolitano(T), Ehud Olmert(W),Anand Panyarachun(W),Helena Paparizou(T),Paris Hilton(F),Sarah Jessica Parker(E),Emma Pierson(E),David Prowse–Vader,Star(E),Romano Prodi(E),Puya Dragoş Gărdescu-La Familia(M),Ted Raimi–Joxer,Xena(W),Donna Reed(M),Keanu Reeves(T),Vladimir Remek(T),Micheline Calmy Rey(E),Rick-battery,Lifehouse(M), Hans Adam Johannes Adam Ferdinand Alois Josef Maria Marko d'Aviano Pius Troppau Jagerndorf Rietberg-sovereign prince(T),Sally Kristen Ride(F),Majel Leigh Hudec Barrett Roddenberry–computer voice,Star Trek(T),Eugene Wesley Gene Roddenberry–director,Star Trek(T),Bako Sahakyan(M),Ivo Sanader(M),Sean–guitar, Lifehouse(E), Shakira Isabel Mebarak Ripoll(M),Elena Helen Hohenzollern Sigmaringen-majesty(T), Radu Hohenzollern Sigmaringen Veringen Duda-vodă(F),Manmohan Singh(M),Fouad Siniora(W),Slash-guitar,Hollywood Roses(E),Irina Spârlea-tennis(F),Britney Spears(T), Winston Baldwin Spencer(F),Frederick Kiefer Rufus,Rachel Sutherland(T),Vlad Irimia Tataee-BUG Mafia(W),Barbara Thompson-sanctity(M),Alexandru Tocilescu(W),Stephen Tompkinson–Danny Trevanion,Wild at Heart(W),Bamir Myrteza Topi(F),Janine Turner-Maggie O'Connell,Northern Exposure(E),Mark Twain(F),Shania Twain(T),Atal Bihari Vajpayee(E),Hassanal Bolkiah Muizzaddin Waddaulah-sultan(M),Taylor Gun Jin Wang (M),Isaiah Washington(E),Alan Wilder-keyboards,drums,Depeche Mode(T),Ramu Yalamanchi(E),Billy Zane(T),Margarita Esther Gómez Campo Calderon Zavala(M),Ian Ziering-Steve,Beverly Hills(E), Tertius Zongo(M), Virginia Zeani Zehan-soprano(E)

The day of the rabbit:

Bryan Adams(m),Andre Kirk Agassi(e),Irakli Alasania(m),Ilham Heydar Oglu Aliyev (m),Thomas Anders-Modern Talking(w),Raluca Ciocârlan Beleşanu Angel-Angels(w), Tony Anholt-Charles Frere,Howards Way(f),Rowan Atkinson-Mr. Bean(f),Ramona Bădescu(w),Ştefan Bănică Junior(t),Elena Băsescu(f),Warren Beatty(e),Kenny Beker-R2,Star(f),Silvia Renate Sommerlath Bernadotte-queen(t),Ernesto Bertarelli(e),Mahesh Bhupathi(e),Bjork Guomundsdottir(e),Andrei Boncea(f),Jessica Bowman-Colleen,Dr. Quinn(w),Lara Flynn Boyle(w),Pierce Brosnan(f),Clifford Lee Burton-guitar,Metallica (e),Francis K Butagira(e),Michael Caine(e),Nicholas Cage(t),Jim Carrey(t),Radu Câmpeanu(f),Dorin Chirtoacă(w),Victor Ciorbea(t),Kim Clijsters(f),Kurt Cobain-Nirvana (t),Jennifer Coolidge(w),Gregory Sean Welts Cuddles–drums,Pyg System(w),Israel Marcel Moshe Blauschild Dalio(m),John Richard Deacon–bass,Queen(m),Dena Delany (e),Rafael Vicente Correa Delgado(e),Marlene Dietrich(e),Dr. Dre André Romelle Young (w),Shannon Doherty-Brenda,Beverly Hills(f),David Duchovny-Fox Mulder,X Files(f), Petru Dugulescu-sanctity(m),Elton Reginald John(w),David Faustino-Bud,Married with Children(w),David Kenneth Roy Thomson Fleet(t),Harrison Ford(f),Jenny Jennifer Frost (t),Peter Gabriel(e),Gaddafi(m),Yuri Alekseyevich Gagarin(e),William Liam John Paul Gallagher-voice,Oasis(t),Harald Glucksburg-king(e),Bear Grylls(e),Daniela Gyorfi(t), Larry Martin Hagman-JR,Dallas(e),Stanley Kirk Burrell MC Hammer(f),Ed Harris(f), Teri Hatcher(m),Jean Heywood(e),Andre Hilgers-drums,Silent Force(w),Susan Howard-Donna,Dallas(m),Alexandrina Hristov(f),Hubert Alexander Ingraham(t),Ephraïm Inoni (f),Yahya Jammeh(e),Wesley Momo Johnson(m),Wei Jingsheng(t),Tony Jones(m), Michael Jordan(m),Michel Kafando(w),Tony Kanal-bass,No Doubt(e),Raj Kapoor(f), Diane Hall Keaton(e),Deborah Kerr(m),Alicia Keys(w),Hossaini Ali Khamenei-seyyed ayatollah(t),Nicole Mary Kidman(t),Nestor Carlos Kirchner(m),Leonard Kleinrock(t), Giovanni Lajolo-cardinal(e),Annie Lennox(t),Yves Camille Désiré Leterme(f),Jack London(e),Mario Lopez-AC Slater,Saved by the Bell(e),Diego Maradona(m),Iuliana Marciuc(f),Steve Stephen Glenn Martin(t),Gates McFadden-Beverly,Star Trek(m),Hans Rudolf Merz(f),Mickael Gorden Thomson-guitar,Pyg System(w),Cristi Minculescu-Iris(m),Matthew Avery Modine(w),Levy Patrick Mwanawasa(m),Jana Nagyova-Arabela(m),Dave Navarro-Red Hot Chili Peppers(w),Ahmed Nazif(t),Jose Maria Pereira Neves(t),John Joseph Jack Nicholson(e),Olusegun Aremu Okikiola Matthew Obasanjo(m),Yoko Ono Lennon(t),Jason Thomas Orange–Take That(m),Anca Parghel(m),James Pickens(t),Kellie Pickler(w),Denine Porter-D12(w),Emilie de Raven (e),Zina Adrianarivelo Azafy(w),Chris Christopher Anton Rea(w),Christina Ricci(t), Michael Richards-Kramer,Seinfeld(t),Marc Rosset(m),Portia de Rossi(f),Mike Rowe(t), Volodymyr Viktor Sabodan-sanctity(w),Henry Gale Sanders-Robert E,Dr. Quinn(w),Jose Eduardo dos Santos(w),Surakiart Sathirathai(t),Al Walid bin Talal Abdul Aziz Al Saud-majesty(f),Jerry Seinfeld-Seinfeld(t),Vandana Shiva(t),Joan Enric Vives i Sicilia-sanctity coprince(t),Alexander Tahir Fadil Siddig Abderahman Mohammed Ahmed Abdel Karim El Mahdi-Julian,Star Trek(e),Haris Silajdzic(w),Margareta Margarita Hohenzollern Sigmaringen Veringen Duda-vodeasă(t),Marcello Spatafora(e),Rod Roderick David Stewart(e),Michael Stipe-REM(m),Theodor Stolojan(t),Mihai Sturzu-Hi Q(w),Siobhan Emma Donaghy–Sugababes(e),Louise Agnetha Lake Tack(m),Ionela Târlea(m),Shirley Temple(w),Neil Frances Tennant(f),Emma Thompson(f),Uma Karuna Thurman(e),Allan Wagner Tizon(m),Tina Turner(f),Bonnie Tyler(e),Helene Udy-Myra,Dr. Quinn(w),Lars Ulrich–drums,Metallica(w),Traciiy Ulrich-guitar,Hollywood Roses(e),Goran Visnic-Kovac Luka,ER(w),Jason Wade-Lifehouse(e),Bruce Willis-David,Moonlighting,5,6(e), Charles Philip Arthur George Wales Windsor-majesty(w),Sean Winfarrah–drums,Inertia (m), Michael York (e), Benazir Bhuto Zardari (w), Catherine Zeta Jones Douglas (w)

The day of the dragon:

Ae Lee(F),Ahmedou Ould Abdallah(E),Mohamed Abdelaziz(E),Roman Abramovich(F), Mahmoud Ahmadinejad(E),Fakhruddin Ahmed(T),Damon Albarn–Blur(W),Tom Anderson(W),Naveen Andrews(W),Clement Athelston Arrindell(T),Sue Baker–tennis(F), Nathalie Baye(W),Ingrid Bergman(W),Albert Bernard El Hadj Omar Ondimba Bongo (M),Andrea Bowen-Julie,Desperate Housewives(E),Judi Bowker-Vicky Gordon,Black Beauty(W),Bucurenci(M),Jennifer Capriati-tennis(M),Leonardo di Caprio(F),Tantoo Cardinal-Snow Bird,Dr. Quinn(F),Joaquim Alberto Chissano(e),Paul Ciuci-Compact(M), Ilarion Ciobanu(F),Helen Elizabeth Clark(W),Frank Collison-Horace,Dr. Quinn(M), Barry Corbin-Maurice,Northern Exposure(W),Nicu Covaci-voice,guitar,Phoenix(E), Mihaela Cernea Craioveanu-voice,Class(T),Howard Ward G Cunningham(F),Dan Bălan Loop-Ozone(T),Brad Delson-guitar,Linkin Park(W),Dan Deneş Dede-Fly Project(T), Alvaro Diez–bass,Dover(T),Stéphane Maurice Dion(W),Ben Diskin(M),Howard Paul Donald–Take That(E),Michael Douglas(W),Tom Dumont-guitar,No Doubt(M), Laurenţiu Duţă–3SE(F),Elena Baltagan-DJ Project(W),Michel Louis Edmond Galabru (E),Ibrahim Agboola Gambari(W),Mircea Geoană(W),Sonja Haraldsen Glucksburg-queen(W),Valerie Jane Morris Goodall(T),Mikhail Sergeyevich Gorbachev Gorbaciov (F),Herbert Grubel(E),Stere Gulea(W),Peter Gyurcsany(T),Gene Hackman (M),Tarja Kaarina Halonen(F),Oeld Mark Hamill-Luke,Star(E),Rona Hartner(T), Abdullah bin Al Hussein Hashemite-king(E),Philip Anthony Hopkins(W),Lucie Jo Hudson–Rosie,Wild at Heart(W),Julian Robert Hunte(F),Jorge Luis Batlle Ibanez(W),Robert Matthew Van Winkle Vanilla Ice(E),Julio Iglesias(F),Joshua Jackson(T),Samuel L Jackson(M), Martinho Ndafa Kabi(W),Ken Kercheval-Cliff,Dallas(W),Chris Klein(M),Zeljko Komsik(E),Mark Knowles–tennis(W),Petr Korda-tennis(W),Michel Kratchvil(T),Jessica Lange (M),Stan Arthur Stanley Jefferson Laurel–Stan Laurel, Laurel and Hardy(E),Aaron Lewis-voice,Staind(E),Chai Ling(T),Kirsti Lintonen(W),Pramukh Swami Maharaj(T), Paul Edgar Philippe Martin Junior(W),Ovidiu Florea Maxx-DJ Project(T),Andie McDowell(E),Mary McDonnell–Dances with Wolves, Galactica(T),Rose McGowan-Paige,Charmed(T),Miloslav Mecir–tennis(E),Andriy Medvedev–tennis(T),Bette Midler (T),Mihai Gruia-Akcent(W),Han Ji Min(W),Thomas Mitchell-the father of Scarlet,Gone with the Wind(T),Muhammad Hosni Mubarak(T),Leonard Simon Nimoy–Spok,Star Trek (M),Ed O'Neill-Al,Married with Children(F),Natasha Sasha Obama(T),Andrés Manuel López El Peje Obrador(E),Leonard Orban(W),Karolos Papoulias(M),Percival Noel James Patterson(F),Mady Patinkin-Jeffrrey,Chicago Hope(M),Andrei Pavel–tennis(E),Arthur Christopher Orme Plummer-The Sound of Music(W),Mekhi Phifer-Gregory Pratt,ER(T), Shawn Pyfrom–Andrew,Desperate Housewives(W),Stat Quo(W),Benedict Ratzinger-pope(M),Tom Noel Rettig-Jeff Miller,Lassie(W),Henrique Pereira Rosa(W),Roxana Andronescu–Popas,Marian Bogdan Todomondo,Capuccino,Spin(E),Ingrid Rubio(M), Viorica Manole(M),Virginia Ruzici–tennis(W),Meg Ryan(F),Lucelia Santos-Isaura(W), Santogold(M),Tigran Sargsyan(F),Aristina Pop Săileanu(E),Steven Segal(M),Vasilache Elena Selena-Candy(F),Nicollette Sheridan-Edie,Desperate Housewives(E),Chen Shuipian Shuibian(M),John Kreuger Hohenzollern Sigmaringen-majesty(T),Alexander Philips Nixon McAteer Hohenzollern Sigmaringen-majesty(T),Igor Nikolaevich Smirnov (T),Andrei Tiberiu Smiley-Simplu(F),Nicéphore Dieudonné Soglo(T),Laszlo Solyom(F), Ian Somerhalder-Boone Carlyle,Lost(F),Kevin David Sorbo–Hercules(T),Cristina Spătar (E),Bruce Joseph Springsteen(F),Violeta Beclea Szekely(M),Boris Tadici(W),Valentina Vladimirovna Tereshkova(W),Tiesto Tijs-DJ(W),Henri Troyat(F),Alexandra Ungureanu (M),Geza Vida(M),Rowan Douglas Williams-sanctity(M), Elisabeth George Bowes Lyon Windsor-queen(M),Philip Edinburgh Windsor-majesty(T),Christian Wolbers Olde-guitar, Arkaea(E), Dwan Jacobsen Young-sanctity(F), Jerry Yang Zhiyuan(M), Zeta-Hi5(M)

The day of the snake:

Jason James Leland Adams - Preston, Dr. Quinn (m), Anil Ambani (f), Amma - devi (m), Monica Anghel(f),Jenniffer Aniston(f),Andres Pastrana Arango(t),Gem Archer-guitar, Oasis(w),Arthur Ashe–tennis(e),Sean Astin–Rudy,Sam,The Lord of the Rings (m),Avi–Activ(t),Juan Evo Morales Ayma(m),Sergei Vasilyevich Bagapsh(w),Gary Barlow–Take That(t),Kim Basinger(w),Halle Maria Barry(t),Shaun Mark Bean–Boromir,The Lord of the Rings(e),Jamie Bell(f),Abdelaziz Belkhadem(m),Jean Paul Belmondo(t),Juliette Binoche(f),Tony Blair(f),Christine Boisson(t),Banjamin Bratt(w),Mihai Budeanu–3SE (t),George Walker Bush(m),C C Catch(m),Robert Cailliau(t),Duane Chase-Kurt,The Sound of Music(m),Tudor Chirilă(e),Lee Van Cleef(w),Mario Cordoso-Henrique,Isaura (e),Dalma Kovacs(f),Donald Watts Davies(f),Cameron Diaz(w),Robert Bobby Digital Diggs RZA-Wu Tang(m),Walt Disney(f),Jamie Draven(m),Francine Fran Joy Drescher (t),Richard Dreyfuss(m),Scott Dunn-voice,guitar,Inertia(t),Clinton Clint Eastwood Junior(m),Douglas Emeron-Scott,Beverly Hills(t),Marshall Bruce Mathers Eminem(m), Ricardo Froilan Lagos Escobar(w),Mihail Formuzal(w),Farrah Franklin-Destiny's Child (m),Noel Thomas David Gallagher-voice,words,guitar,Oasis(w),Mihai Emil Georgescu (t),Richard Tiffany Gere(w),Mel Columcille Gerard Gibson(e),Giulia Anghelescu-Candy(t),Martin Gore-Depeche Mode(f),Jean-Marie Guéheno(w),Teofisto Guingona Junior(t),Cristina Haioş(e),Geraldine Geri Estelle Halliwell–Spice Girls(e),Egumena Benedicta Grigore-sanctity(f),Tom Hamilton-bass,Aerosmith(t),Woody Harrelson(f), Brian Lee Harvey-East17(m),Dirty Harry-D12(m),Doris Hart-tennis(f),Dennis Haskins-Belding,Saved by the Bell(f),Şerban Hienă-AnimalX(m),Leslie Howard-Asley,Gone with the Wind(e),Felicity Huffman-Lynette,Desperate Housewives(m),Natalie Jane Imbruglia(m),Mahalia Jackson(e),Michaelle Jean(m),Wyclef Jean(m),Angelina Jolie (m),Petr Kellner(e),Mohammad Khazaee(w),Christine Lahti-Kate,Chicago Hope(e), James Jay Leno(w),Amparo Llanos–guitar,Dover(m),Petru Chiril Lucinschi(e),Augustine Philip Mahiga(p),Martziano-guitar,Animal X(f),Mark Allan Hoppus-Blink182(t),John McEnroe-tennis(e),Swifty McVay-D12(e),Colm O Maonaigh Meaney–Miles,Star Trek (m),Peter Medgyessy(t),Stjepan Stipe Mesic(e),Jesse Metcalfe-John Rowland, Desperate Housewives(t),Patricia Millardet–Silvia Conti,La Piovra(t),Lakshmi Narayan Mittal(m), Nana Ioanna Mouskouri(f),Jean Eyeghe Ndong(f),Sergiu Nicolaescu(w),Jana Novotna-tennis(t),Barack Hussein Obama(e),Kelly Osbourne(w),Nemesi Marques Oste-sanctity (w),Samuel Otsile Outlule(m),Glyn Owen–Jack Rolfe,Howards' Way(t),Mark Anthony Patrick Owen-Take That(f),Paul Dedrick Gray-bass,Pyg System(e),Oscar Berger Perdomo(f),Jean Ping(m),Michele Placido–Corrado Cattani,La Piovra(w),Călin Pop-voice,Celelalte cuvinte(m),Andrew Lee Potts(e),Marin Preda(t),Priscillla Ann Beaulieu Presley–Jenna,Dallas(w),Randy Quaid(e),Mimi Rogers Miriam Spickler(w),Robyn Rihanna Fenty(t),Ronaldinho Ronaldo de Assis Moreira(w),Jose Manuel Zelaya Rosales (e),Isa Rossellini(t),Dave Rowttree-drums,Blur(f),Alexander Rybak(f),Pete Sampras(e), Serzh Azati Sargsyan(f),Katharine Jefferts Schori-sanctity(m),Seal Sealhenry Olusegun Olumide Adelo Samuel(w),Kamalesh Sharma(m),Thaksin Shinawatra(f),Sergey Sidorsky (e),Casimir Mystkowski Hohenzollern Sigmaringen-majesty(w),Hose Alencar Gomes da Silva(t),Jose Socrates Sousa(m),Sylvester Stallone(m),Patrick Stewart-Jean Luc Picard, Star Trek(f),Quentin Tarantino(e),Vasilica Tastaman(t),Roger Meddows Taylor–drums, Queen(f),Shirley Jane Temple(w),Tom Thomas Matthew DeLonge-Blink182(w),Amadou Toumani Touré(w),John Joseph Travolta(t),Mihai Trăistariu(f),Robert Trujillo-bass,Metallica(t),Ivana Marie Zelnickova Trump(m),Matti Taneli Vanhanen(e),Alan White–drums,Oasis(f),Megan Mingyu Williams–Cassie,Return to Eden(m),Wuerkaixi (f), Andreea Berecleanu Zaharescu (l), Toth Zoltan Zoli – Sistem (m), China Zorrilla (m)

The day of the horse:

Anda Adam-RACLA(M), Lal Krishna Kishenchand Advani(F), Adewale Akinnouye Agbaje-Eko,Lost(E),Alexander Aleksandr Zolotinskovich Ankvab(F),Kofi Annan(M), Bernard Arnault(T),Meles Legesse Zenawi Asres(M),Roger Bart-George,Desperate Housewives(M),Vali Bărbulescu–DJ,singer(M),Ioana Băsescu(T),Amanda Bearse-Marcy,Married with Children(E),Harry Belafonte(T),Carlos Filipe Ximenes Belo-sanctity(E),Josie Bisset(E),Rufus Bizare-D12(E),Bobi-Fără Zahăr(E),Dieter Bohlen–Modern Talking(E),Laura Lane Welch Bush(W),Mariah Carey(F),Cher Cherilyn Sarkisian(T),Jacques René Chirac-president coprince(T),Chelsea Victoria Clinton(M), James Coco(M),Phil Collins-Genesis(M),David Crystal-guitar,voice,piano,drums,The Doo Doo Heads(W),John Paul Cusack(E),Hilario Gelbolingo Davide Junior(M),Marlin Jim Davis-Jock,Dallas(E),Viktoras Diawara-voice,guitar,Skamp(F),Said Djinnit(T),Jean Jacques Dordain(E),Julia Louis Dreyfus-Elaine,Seinfeld(F),Patrick Duffy-Bobby,Dallas (F),James Eckhouse-Brend's dad,Beverly Hills(F),Anthony Edwards-Green,ER(E), Shannon Elizabeth-Nadia,American Pie(F),Agnetha Ase Faltskog-ABBA(M),Roger Federer-tennis(E),Ralph Nathaniel Twisleton Wykeham Fiennes(T),Jane Jayne Seymour Fonda(W),Claude Jeanne Malca Gensac(T),Louis Germain David de Funès de Galarza(E),Jorge Garcia-Hugo,Lost(T),Elena Gheorghe-Mandinga(M),Rebecca Gilling–Stephanie Harper,Return to Eden(E),John Herschel Glenn Junior(W),Călin Goia-voice,Voltaj(M),Geneviève Grad(M),Linda Gray-Sue Ellen,Dallas(E),Paul McGuigan Guigsy–bass,Oasis(T),Alec Guiness–Obi,Star(E),Arthur Dion Hanna(F),Stephen Joseph Harper(W),John Carter Hensley(E),Carlos Slim Helu(M),Martina Hingis(F),Baki Ilkin(T),Laura Innes-Kerry Weaver,ER(M),Julia Dolly Joiner(W),Juvenile(M),Ingvar Feodor Kamprad(E),Hamid Karzai(M),Edward Kerr-James Brody,SeaQuest(F),Daniel Dae Kim-Jin Kwon,Lost(F),Julie Tawny Kitaen–Deianira,Hercules(M),Yao Roland Kpotsra(M),Jude Law(T),Lucy Liu(F),Sophia Loren(T),Alexander Lukashenko(E),David Lynch–director,Twin Peaks(T),John Malkovich(T),Robert Bob Nesta Marley(F),Chris Martin-Coldplay(E),Liz McClarnon(E),Fernando Armindo Lugo Mendez(M),Natalie Jackson Mendoza–Jackie Clunes,Hotel Babylon(F),Freddy Farrokh Bulsara Mercury-voice,Queen(W),Dominic Monaghan-Charlie,Lost(T),Fernanda Montenegro(T),The Mosh(M),Knight Robert Mugabe(M),Paul Nathan-Robert Cheadle,ER(W),Ilie Năstase (T),Ne-Yo(E),Jason Newsted-bass,Metallica(F),Krist Novoselio–bass,Nirvana(M),Sandra Oh-Cristina Yang,Grey's Anatomy(F),Juhan Parts(E),Harold Perrineau-Michael Dawson, Lost(W),Peg Phillips-Ruth Anne Miller,Northern Exposure(M),Alison Pill (M),Pedro Verona Rodrigues Pires(M),Natalie Portman-Amidala,Star(E),Carol Potter-Brend's mum,Beverly Hills,90210(F),Anthony Quinn(W),Regina Jonas–rabbina(E),Molly Ringwald(E),Tara Reid-Vicky,American Pie(E),Cristina Rus-Blondy(M),Răzvan Sabău-tennis player(F),Eveline Widmer Schlumpf(W),Eric Emerson Schmidt(E),Jordan-Scooter (M),Ilia Irakli Gudushauri Shiolashvili-patriarch(M),Ana Anne Antoinette Françoise Charlotte of Bourbon Parma Charles Ferdinand Hohenzollern Sigmaringen-queen(T), Nicolae Nicholas Mihai Michael Medforth Mills Hohenzollern Sigmaringen-majesty(M), Paul Filip Philippe Hohenzollern Sigmaringen-majesty(M),Ellen Johnson Sirleaf(T),Sişu Tudor-La Familia(W),Li Ka Shing(M),Roosevelt Skerrit(M),Kevin Tod Smith–Ares, Xena(E),Wesley Snipes(M),Zack Starkey–drums,Oasis(M),Gary Lewis Stevenson (F), Byron Stroud-bass,Arkaea(E),Peter Strauss(M),Donald McNichol Sutherland(T),Viorel Şipoş-3SE(W),Jalal Talabani(W),Horia Tecău(E),Margaret Hilda Roberts Thatcher(M), Mirek Topolanek(W),Mary Kathleen Turner(F),Elizabeth Taylor(E),Ion Țiriac(F),Joao Bernardo Nino Vieira(T),Lucian Viziru(F),Denzel Hayes Washington Junior(E),Elijah Jordan Wood(F), Alfre Woodard-Betty,Desperate Housewives(E), Renée Zellweger(M)

The day of the sheep:

Isaias Afewerki(f),AJ Alexander James-Backstreet Boys(m),Alex Velea(f),Jonelle Allen-Grace,Dr. Quinn(w),Sergio Miguel Andrade-bass,Lifehouse(f),Jesus Antunes-drums, Dover(t),Stephen Baldwin(m),Rupiah Banda(m),Baron Cohen(m),Elizabeth Berkley-Jesie,Saved by the Bell(e),Orlando Bloom(e),Bobo-Fără Zahăr(m),Ion Mihai Botean-sanctity(m),Raoul Bova–Gianni,La Piovra(m),Jonathan Brandis–Lucas,SeaQuest(t), Mahcad Brooks-Matthew,Desperate Housewives(m),Levar Burton-Geordi La Forge, Star Trek(e),Steven Vincent Buscemi(e),Barbara Pierce and Jenna Welch Bush(f), Francisco Javier Arias Cardenas(e),Gabrielle Carteris-Andrea Zackerman,Beverly Hills, 90210(t),Michael Chang(w),Chadd Channing-drums,Nirvana(t),Sean Connery(f),Jacques Yves Cousteau(f),Răzvan Crivaci Krivach(t),Branko Crvenkovski(w),Macaulay Culkin (m),Dalai Tenzin Gyatso-lama(w),Hope Davis(m),Suzanne Pierrette Delaire(f),Denisa-Bambi(t),Oleg Deripaska(m),Devvarman(w),Sean John Combs Puffy Daddy Diddy(w), Mark Sinclair Vincent Vin Diesel(w),Mike Michael Ryan Pritchard Dirnt-bass,Greenday (t),Mswati Makhosetive Dlamini-king(e),Kirsten Caroline Dunst(w),Christopher Eccleston-Doctor Who(t),Rubens de Falco-Leoncio,Isaura(f),Farrell(w),François Fillon (e),Lady Gaga(m),David Gahan-Depeche Mode(f),David Garrisson-Steve, Married with Children(f),Greg Germann(t),Luis Alfredo Palacio Gonzalez(e),Michael Douglas Griffin (t),Florin Grozea-Hi Q(t),Nikola Gruevski(w),Vladimer Lado Gurgenidze(m),Rania Al Yassin Hashemite-queen(w),Raymond Herrera-drums,Arkaea(w),Tommy Haas-tennis(t), Jennifer Low Hewitt(e),Sam Samuel Archibald Anthony Hinds(e),Michael Eric Hurst–Iolaus,Hercules(t),Jeremy Irons(f),Murat Iusuf-mufti(f),LL Cool J James Todd Smith(w), Bharrat Jagdeo(m),Alex James-bass,Blur(t),Wen Jiabao Chiapao(m),Howard Harold Clifford Keel-Clayton,Dallas,7(t),Monica Keena(t),Keo Cosmin Mustață(e),Yunjin Kim-Sun,Lost(f),Brent and Shane Kinsman-Preston and Porter,Deperate Housewives(e), Robert Sedraki Kocharyan(e),Nouradine Delwa Kassiré Koumakoye(t),Brian Krause(f), Ravi Meir Lau-rabbi(e),Doris Leuthard(w),Nicholas Joseph Orville Liverpool(w),Cristina Llanos-voice,Dover(w),Chris Lowe(e),Ludacris Brian Bridges(m),Ricky Martin(w),Eric Martin–Technotronic(m),Koichiro Matsura(e),Mathew David McCanaughey(w),Ted McGinley-Jeff,Married with Children(f),Vashti Murphy McKenzie-sanctity(f),Dmitry Anatolyevich Medvedev(m),Cornell Haynes Nelly(f),Pierre Nkurunziza(t),Renée Evelyn O'Connor–Gabrielle,Xena(m),Barbara O'Neil-the mother of Scarlet,Gone with the Wind (w),Peter O'Toole(t),Laurence Olivier(m),Haley Joel Osment(t),Irene Lelekou Papas (t),Georgi Sedefchov Parvanov(m),Andre Patton-Outkast(f),Joe Robert Pemagbi(t),Maria Eva Duarte Peron(e),Shimon Szymon Peres Perski(f),Pharrell Williams(m),William Bradley Brad Pitt(t),Sellapan Ramanathan(w),Charles Rabemananjara(e),Pierre Richard (e),Tatavia Robertson-voice,Linkin Park(m),Tabare Ramon Vazquez Rosas(e),Mikheil Saakashvili(e),Adam Sandler(m),Alan Bartlett Shepard Junior(t),Alain Michel Léonce Biarneix Hohenzollern Sigmaringen-majesty(w),Angelica Margareta Bianca Kreuger Hohenzollern Sigmaringen-majesty(f),Mihai Michael Torsten Kreuger Hohenzollern Sigmaringen-majesty(t),Leslie Robin Medforth Mills Hohenzollern Sigmaringen-majesty (t),Gilles Simon(t),Rosny Smarth(t),Jimmy Smits(m),Mircea Snegur(e),Alina Sorescu(e), Marin Sorescu(m),Mira Sorvino(t),Laura Stoica(f),Maryl Streep(w),Barbara Streisand (f),Sherry Stringfield-Susan,ER(e),Hippolyte Taine(f),Constantin Călin Anton Popescu Tăriceanu(e),Luis Tosar(m),Turturo(m),Liv Rundgren Tyler(e),Timotei Ursu(e),Ronald Venetiaan(m),Guillermo Vilas(t),John Voight(t),Damon Wayans(t),Sigourney Weaver (m),Henri Albert Gabriel Félix Marie Guillaume Bourbon Parma Nassau Weilburg-grand duke(f),Serena Jameka Williams(f),Diana Frances Wales Windsor-princess(t),Youcef Yousfi(w),Oana Zăvoranu(w),Zhang Ziyi(f),Adrian Zmed(e),Denis Zmeu(f),JZ Zuma(t)

The day of the monkey:

Ulf-Ace of Base(M),Adam-Maroon5(T),Adina Postelnicu-Heaven(M),Akon Thiam(F), Lalla Salma Bennani Cherif Sharif Alaouite-majesty(W),Mohammed Al Hafiz Al Sayyid Al Hassan Cherif Sharif Alaouite-king(F),Jason Alexander-George Constanza,Seinfeld (E),Paul Gardner Allen(W),Emeka Anyaoku(T),Billie Joe Amstrong-Green Day(W), Emeka Anyaoku(T),Tracy Austin-tennis(T),Traian Băsescu(E),Monica Bârlădeanu(E), Elizabeth Berkley(M),Natasha Anne Bedingfield(E),Norma Blum-Malvina,Isaura(W), Paul Arthurs Bonehead-guitar,Oasis(E),Avery Franklin Brooks-Benjemin Sisko,Star Trek (M),Rosa Isabel Mutya Buena-Sugababes(M),Emma Lee Bunton-Spice Girls(W),Richard Burgi-Karl,Desperate Housewives(E),Kate Bush(E),Neve Campbell(W),Cristian Chivu (W),Jean Loup Jacques Marie Chrétien(T),Emil Constantinescu(M),Cooper-Silent Force (E),Cosmin-Cassa Loco(E),Victor Valentin Crivoi(E),Wang Dan(W),Andrei Dapkiunas (T),Patrick Dempsey-Derek,Grey's Anatomy(W),Adrian Despot-Vița de Vie(W),Jay Dittamo,Junoon(T),Phesheya Mbongeni Dlamini(M),Dida Drăgan(F),Milo Dukanovic (T),Bob Dylan(W),Tsakhiagiin Elbegdorj(W),Gareth John Evans(W),Stacy Ann Fergie Ferguson(W),Fernand Joseph Désiré Contandin Fernandel(F),Franck Gérard Contandin Fernandel(M),Sally Field(T),Theodor Fontane(W),John Frusciante–guitar,RHCP(T), Hannz G-D12(F),Barbara Bel Geddes-Ellie,Dallas(W),Geru(T),Susan Gilmore–Avril, Howards' Way(T),Olafur Ragnar Grimsson(W),Joshua Daniel Hartnett(T),Albert Félix Humbert Théodore Christian Eugène Marie Saxe Coburg Gotha-king(E),Steffi Stefanie Maria Graf Agassi(M),Kirk Hammett-guitar,Metallica(M),Jimi Hendrix(T),Amanda Holden-Sarah Trevanion,Wild at Heart(W),Josh Holloway-James Ford,Lost(F),Whitney Houston(T),Victor Hugo(F),Veronica Michelle Bachelet Jeria(W),Hu Jintao(E),James Earl Jones-voice Vader,Star(W),Joseph Kabila Kabange(M),Costas Kostas Konstantinos Alexandrou Caramanlis Karamanlis(T),Kelis Rogers Jones(M),Khalifah bin Salman Al Khalifah(E),Shahrukh Khan(M),Martin Luther King Junior-sanctity(M),Padma Parvati Lakshmi(T),Marius Lăcătuş(T),Monica Samille Lewinsky(M),Jerry Lee Lewis(E),Leona Louise Lewis(E),Elisabeta Lipă–canoer(E),Eva Longoria-Gabrielle Solis,Desperate Housewives(M),Peter MacNicol-John,Ally McBeal(F),Ferenc Madl(T),Roma Maffia(E), Christian Marin(T),Vicki Fujii Matsumori-sanctity(T),Joey McIntyre-New Kids on the Block(F),Duff McKagan-bass,Hollywood Roses(T),Coleen Kent Menlove-sanctity (M),Celestino Migliore-sanctity(E),Alyssa Milano(T),Ahmed Ali Al Mirghani(F),Ban Ki Moon(E),Pat Morita(M),Mark Moses-Paul,Desperate Housewives(W),Murdoc-Gorillaz (F),Parminder Nagra-Neela,ER(T),Kim Yong Nam(T),Giorgio Napolitano(T),Marc Nelson-BoyzIIMen(E),Thomas Ian Nicholas(T),Alexa Niculae(T),Ishmael Noko-sanctity (M),Leander Adrian Paes(T),Maxim Palmer-MC,The Prodigy(T),Ivan Patzaichin-canoeist(M),Joe Perry-guitar,Aerosmith(E),Édith Piaf(T),Billie Piper-Rose,Doctor Who(E),Emilia Popescu(M),Robert Powell(F),Elvis Presley(T),Daniel Radcliffe-Harry Potter(T),Torsten Rohre-piano,Silent Force(E),Joseph Yule Mickey Rooney(T),Kelendria Trene Rowland-Destiny's Child(M),Dumitru Rucăreanu(F),Kevin Michael Rudd(F),Bob Robert Lane Saget-Danny,Full House(T),Stavrofora Teofana Scântei-sanctity(W),Fatmir Sejdiu(F),Ayrton Senna(E),Mizan Zainal Wathiqu Tuanku Abidin Ibni Marhum Mahmud Al Muktafi Billah Shah-sultan(M),Charlie Sheen(M),Kayo Shekoni(F),Cybill Shepherd-Maddie,Moonlighting(T),Lia Georgia Triff Hohenzollern Sigmaringen-majesty(T),Chad Smith-drums,RHCP(F),Han Seung Soo(T),Michael Imperioli Soprano(M),Shawn Patrick Stockman-Boyz II Men(M),Hillary Swank(W),Peta Tappano-Jilly,Return to Eden(T), Richard Thomas(T),Jennifer Tilly(F),Shakur Amaru Tupac(W),Mike Tyson(M),Heraldo Munoz Valenzuela(E),Vierme-AnimalX(F),Filip Vujanovic(M),Jiang Wen(E),Noah Whyle – John Carter, ER (M), Kate Winslet (T), Gheorghe Zamfir (T), Leyla Zana (F)

The day of the rooster:

Edward Fenech Adami(e),Mahamat Ali Adoum(f),Carlos Alberto Chacho Alvarez(t), John D'Aquino–Benjemin,SeaQuest(m),Mukesh Ambani(m),Tori Amos(f),Nguyen Van An(m),Raed Arafat-SMURD(w),David Frederick Attenborough(f),George Gigi Becali(w),Barbara Babcock-Dorothy,Dr. Quinn(t),Amitabh Bachchan(f),Natalia Barbu (m),Andreea Violeta Marin Bănică(f),Maria Băsescu(e),Benjamin-Outkast(w),Beyoncé Beyincé Giselle Knowles(t),Betty-Etnic(m),Juan Carlos Glucksburg Bourbon-king(f),Ion Caramitru(m),Manuel Leuterio Noli de Castro Junior(f),Bhumibol Adulyadej Chakri-king(w),Sirikit Mom Rajawongse Sirikit Kitiyakara Chakri-queen(t),Richard Charles–Oliver Twist(w),Ştefan Ion Cătălin Cheloo-Paraziţii(t),André Chéret(t),Minoru Chiaki (w),Tracey Childs–Lynne,Howards' Way(w),Jonathan Chimier(m),Chris-drums,Pyg System(t),Vitaly Ivanovich Churkin(f),Nadia Comăneci(e),Holly Marie Combs-Pieper, Charmed(w),Vitalii Cozari-Millenium(e),Michael Crichton-director,ER(e),O'Shea Jackson Ice Cube(m),Matt Damon(m),Terry Terence Anthony Gordon Davis(f),David Howell Evans The Edge–guitar,U2(w),Cary Elwes(f),Nambaryn Enkhbayar(e),Nicolas Escudé(t),Mia Farrow(e),Carrie Fisher-Leila,Star(m),Isla Lang Fisher(t),Erika Flores-Colleen,Dr. Quinn(w),Jonathan Frakes-William Ricker,Star Trek(f),Hugo Rafael Chavez Frias(t),Andres Garcia(w),Glen Glose(f),Nora Gorbe-Linda(w),Loredana Groza Boncea-singer(m),Abdullah Gul(f),Oliver Norvell Hardy–Bran Hardy,Laurel and Hardy(e), Carmen Mureşan Harra-Trio Expres(t),Audrey Kathleen Ruston Hepburn(e),Katherine Houghton Hepburn(m),Angelica Huston(e),Leo Iorga-Pacifica(t),Ivan Janez Jansa(f), Philip Michael Jeffery(w),Dominique Strauss Kahn(l),Paul Kasey–Cyber Leader,Doctor Who(w),George Kennedy-McKay,Dallas(w),Kevin Scott Richardson-Backstreet Boys (m),Zalmay Mamozy Khalilzad(m),Seretse Khama Ian Khama(e),Ben Kingsley(m), Jordan Nathaniel Marcel Knight–New Kids on the Block(f),T.R.Knight–George O'Malley,Grey's Anatomy(m),Junichiro Koizumi(m),Joey Kramer-drums,Aerosmith(f), Svetlana Kuznetsova(f),Gina Lallabrigida(e),Lorenzo Lamas(f),Larry Mullen-drums,U2 (f),Jean François Lécureux(m),Roger Lécureux(m),John Lennon-The Beatles(t),Leonard-Cassa Loco(e),Heather Locklear(m),Shelley Long(t),Geoffrey Lower–Timothy,Dr.Quinn (m),Sue Lyon(t),Marius Nedelcu-Akcent(w),Steve McQueen(w),Marilyn Monroe(m), Amélie Moresmo(w),Alanis,Imre Morissette(w),Pranab Kumar Mukherjee(m),Michael Obiora–Ben Trueman,Hotel Babylon(t),Gary Oldman(f),Jamie Oliver(w),Oprah Winfrey (t),Lawrence Edward Page(m),Gwyneth Paltrow(m),Bud Spencer Carlo Pedersoli-Piedonne(e),Mary Pierce(m),Cédric Pioline(m),Sidney Poitier(t),Adela Elena Popescu(t), Christopher Reeve(w),Brian Trick B Rock-Backstreet Boys(f),Petre Roman(f),Nikolay Romanov-majesty(f),Ronaldo Luis Nazario de Lima(w),Ali Abdullah Saleh(w),Letsie David Mohato Bereng Seeiso-king(m),Masenate Mohato Motsoeneng Anna Karabo Seeiso-queen(t),Alberto Selva(w),Ariel Sharon Scheinermann(f),Mihai Michael Bourbon Parma Carol Charles Ferdinand Hohenzollern Sigmaringen-king(m),Scott Raynor–Blink 182(t),Imbarek Shamekh(m),Brooke Shields(t),Michael Thomas Somare(m),Kevin Spacey(e),Narcisa Suciu(w),Nicolae Oncescu Swamp-BUG Mafia(e),David Tenant–The Doctor,Doctor Who(w),Randall Justin Timberlake(e),Herman Andimba Toivo ya Toivo (w),Josefa Iloilovatu Uluivuda(m),Usher Raymond(e),Eugenia Vodă(t),Vladimir Nicolae Voronin(w),Marky Mark Robert Michael Wahlberg(m),Richard William Wil Wheaton–Wesley,Star Trek(m),Michelle Williams-Destiny's Child(f),Robbie Williams–Take That (t),Venus Ebony Starr Williams(m),Camilla Cornwall Rothesay Rosemary Shand Parker Bowles Wales Windsor-majesty(f),Richard Wurmbrand-sanctity(f),Ma Ying Jeou Yingjeou Yingjiu Yingchiu(e),François Bozizé Yangouvonda(m),Adrian Young-drums, No Doubt(w), Colville Norbert Young(t), Milla Yovovich(f), Zinedine Yazid Zidane(t)

The day of the dog:

Inga Brit Monica Stigsdotter Ahlenius(F),Daniel Albineri–Jake,Return to Eden (T),Alina Diana–ASIA(W),Julie Julia Elizabeth Wells Andrews-Maria,The Sound of Music(M), Luminița Anghel-singer(M),Aksoltan Torayewna Atayewa(T),Bacon Bros(F),Massoud Barzani(W),Ion Bazac(E),Carl Folke Hubertus Gustaf Bernadotte-king(T),Jason Biggs (T),Paul Biya(M),Joseph Nyumah Boakai(E),BoBo Peter-Dj(T),Sam Bobrick-director, Saved by the Bell(F),Paul David Hewson Bono-U2(E),Sofia Glucksburg Bourbon-queen (E),Sarah Brightman(T),Richard Burton(E),George Herbert Walker Bush Senior(W), Alvaro Colom Caballeros(F),Eugène Camara(T),Blu Tiffany Cobb Cantrell(F),Renée Annie Nina Cassian(M),Fidel Castro(T),Darius Cekuolis(M),Noel Clarke–Mickey, Doctor Who(F),Blaise Compaoré(T),Tre Cool Frank Edwin Wright-drums,Green Day(T), Corina Ciorbă(E),Graham Coxon-guitar,Blur(F),Claudia Pavel-Candy,Cream(F),Marcia Cross-Bree,Desperate Housewives(W),Russel Crowe(F),Cindy Crowford(M),Steven Culp-Rex,Desperate Housewives(E),Gérard Xavier Marcel Depardieu(F),Brandon Douglas Sokolosky-Andrew,Dr. Quinn(W),Enya Eithne Patricia Ni Bhraonain Brennan(M),Christine Estabrook-Martha,Desperate Housewives(W),Sherilyn Fenn(F), Heinz Fischer(T),Florin-Amicii,Marfar(M),Matthew Fox-Jack Shephard,Lost(T),Nelly Kim Furtado(E),Clark Gable-Rhett,Gone with the Wind(M),Bill Gates(W),Cynthia Geary-Shelley,Northern Exposure(T),Boutros Boutros Ghali(F),Syed Makhdoom Yousaf Raza Gillani(F),Antoine Gizenga(W),Elias Antonio Saca Gonzalez(W),Abel Nguéndé Goumba(M),Virgil Ivan Gus Grissom(W),Ismaïl Omar Guelleh(M),Bug Hall(T),Andrew Hanson-guitar,Inertia(M),Mark Hanson-sanctity(M),Nicholas Hammond-Fredrick,The Sound of Music(M),Lee Kun Hee(W),John Hendricks(T),Jonathan John Darren Hendy–East17(M),Carmen Maria Gallardo Hernandez(W),Yoshio Inaba(T),Marcel Iureş(T), Patricia Kaas(E),Charles Kuen Kao(T),Ted King-Andrew,Charmed(E),Vaclav Klaus(E), Samuel Kobia-sanctity(E),Chung Mong Koo(M),John Kufi Agyekum Kufuor(T),Lucy Lawless Lucille Frances Ryan-Xena(E),Bruce Lee(T),Moritz Leuenberger(E),Pascal Lissouba(T),Wangari Muta Maathai(T),Jawad Nouri Kamel Al Maliki(F),Marcello Mastroianni(M),Mbela Nzuzi-Gloria(T),Mary McAleese(E),Julian McMahon-Cole, Charmed(E),Ray Mears(F),Angela Dorothea Kasner Merkel(T),Hayley Mills–Caroline, Wild at Heart(W),Kylie Ann Minogue(E),Jeanne Moreau(W),Nathan Bartholomew Morris–Boyz II Men(T),Rob Morrow-Joel Fleichman,Northern Exposure(T),Anthony Tony Michael Mortimer–East 17(T),Mihnea Ioan Motoc(T),Claus Jonkheer Amsberg Orange Nassau-majesty(E),Nursultan Abishuly Nazarbayev(M),Paul Newman(M),Terry O'Quinn-John,Lost(W),Ioana Olaru-tennis(W),Michael Ontkean-Harry,Twin Peaks(E), Ozzy Osbourne(W),Al Pacino(E),Luke Perry(E),Adrian Pintea(E),Priscilla Presley(F), Victoria Principal-Pamela,Dallas(f),Om Puri(F),Vladimir Putin(F),Mihaela Rădulescu (M),Condoleezza Rice(T),Ioan Robu-sanctity(T),Eriq la Salle-Peter,ER(W),Roy Schneider–Nathan,Seaquest(T),Baxxter-Scooter(T),Joan Severance(T),Jane Seymour-Michaela,Dr. Quinn(F),Maria Sharapova(E),Takashi Shimura(M),Shirazinia-Deep Dish (T),Irina Irene Hohenzollern Sigmaringen-majesty(M),Maria Ileana Kottulinsky Lorraine Habsburg Hohenzollern Sigmaringen-majesty(T),Sofia Sophie Hohenzollern Sigmaringen-majesty(T),Bob Christophe Le Friant Sinclar(T),Stan Smith(W),Will Smith (E),Mian Soomro(F),Ferdi Sabit Soyer(M),Nikola Spiric(T),Amelle Berrabah–Sugababes (F),Arnold Swartzeneger(M),Șopârlă-AnimalX(W),Klaus Topfer(W),Tudor Ionescu-Fly Project(T),Steven Tyler-Aerosmith(M),Tzapu-bass,AnimalX(M),Tzetze-AnimalX(M), Kate Voegele(F),Amina Wadud-imama(T),Kate Walsh-Addison,Grey's Anatomy,Private Practice(M),Hugo Wallace Weaving(W),Robin Williams(W),Chandra Wilson(T),Mara Wilson(T), Timothy Wirth(W), Lee Li Xianlong(F), Alvin Joiner Nathaniel Xzibit(W)

The day of the pig:

Iajuddin Ahmed(f),Woody Allen(m),Prakash Amritraj-tennis(w),Andra Alexandra Irina Mihai Măruţă-singer(e),Ricardo Alberto Arias(m),Neil Alden Armstrong(f),Adrian Pleşca Artan-Timpuri Noi,Partizan(w),Kurmanbek Saliyevich Bakiyev(w),Orson Bean-Loren,Dr. Quinn(W),Allyce Beasley-Agnes,Moonlighting(w),Andy Andrew Piran Bell-bass,Oasis(w),Rob Bouron-drums,Linkin Park(f),David Bowie(f),Mel B–Spice Girls(t), Mel Gro Harlem Brundtland(f),Barbara Pierce Bush(w),Busta Rhymes(m),Kelly Carlson(e),Ryan Carnes-Justin,Desperate Housewives(w),James Caviezel(e),The Cheeky Girls(f),Dimitris Christofias(t),Daniel Ciobotea-patriarch(w),George Clooney(e), Terence Terry Mark Coldwell–East 17(w),John Collums-Holling,Northern Exposure(m), Judith Craig-sanctity(w),Mary Crosby-Kristin,Dallas(e),Penelope Cruz(e),James Denton-Mike, Desperate Housewives(w),Minnie Driver(m),Margit Binder Fischer(f),Petre Urda Freakadadisk-Paraziţii(e),Oscar Nicanor Duarte Frutos(m),Jean Gabin(m),Cary Grant(m), Dorian Gregory-Darryl,Charmed(m),Nigel Davenport–Edward,Howard's Way(w),Jan Harvey-Howard's Way(m),Tamer Hassan(f),Olivia de Havilland-Melanie,Gone with the Wind(e),Benny Hill(e),Zane Huett-Parker,Desperate Housewives(m),Janice Riggle Huie-sanctity(w),Roxanne Hurt-Camille Dushene Shutt,ER(t),Lubomyr Husar-cardinal(w), Irina Nicolae-ASIA(w),Janet-Jacksons(t),Jon Bon Jovi(e),Joy Lauren- Danielle,Desperate Housewives(m),Hamad bin Isa Al Khalifa-king(w),Antoine Karam(f),Steve Steven Francis Kanaly-Ray,Dallas(f),Jakaya Mrisho Kikwete(t),Val Kilmer(f), Solange Piages Knowles-Destiny's Child(e),Horst Köhler(m),Vojislav Kostunica(f),Lenny Kravitz(t), Burt Lancaster(f),Luis Lazarus(t),Jet Li Lianjie(e),Kyle MacLchlan-Dale,Twin Peaks(t), Martin Marquez–Gino Primola,Hotel Babylon(m),Brian Harold May–guitar,Queen(e), George Michael(e),Sania Mirza(w),François Maurice Adrien Marie Mitterrand-president coprince(e),Antonio Ermirio de Moraes(t),Maia Morgenstern(e),Adrian Mutu(t),Beatrix Amsberg Orange Nassau-queen(w),Adrian Neritani(w),Nick Nolte(f),Ene Noni(w), Adrian Paul(m),Pele(e),Hans Gert Pottering(f),Jason Priestly-Brandon,Beverly Hills(t), Amfilohije Radovic-patriarch(e),Leonel Antonio Fernandez Reyna(m),Burt Reynolds(w), Joely Kim Richardson(w),Alexius Ridiger-patriarch(e),Marie Aglae Kinsky Wchinitz Tettau Rietberg-majesty(f),Kimmy Robertson-Lucy Moran,Twin Peaks(f),Romina Francesca Power(t),Cristiano Ronaldo(t),Axl William Bruce Rose–voice,Hollywood Roses(t),Stefanic Oszkar Osi Rudolf Rudi-Activ(w),Dimitrij Rupel(m),Winona Ryder (f),Marat Safin–tennis(e),Katey Sagal–Peggy,Married with Children(t),Edouard Victor Saouma(e),Larry Lawrence Mark Sanger(f),Jacky Sangster–Culture Beat(w),Fernando da Piedade Nando Dias dos Santos(e),Susan Abigail Tomalin Sarandon(m),Anand Satch Satyanand(f),Telly Savalas(e),Choummaly Sayasone(f),Roy Scheider–Nathan Bridger, SeaQuest(t),Samuel Schmid(f),Gyanendra Jnanendra Bir Vira Bikram Vikrama Shah Dev Sahadeva Shah-king(f),Vonda Shepard-music,Ally McBeal(m),Mike Shinoda-voice, Linkin Park(e),William Shockley–Hank Lawson,Dr. Quinn(w),Akihito Showa-emperor (w),Than Shwe(e),Maria Hohenzollern Sigmaringen-majesty(w),Elisabeta Maria Bianca Elena Biarneix Hohenzollern Sigmaringen-majesty(e),Leo Cook Fatboy Slim(t),Juan Somavia(e),Guillaume Kigbafori Soro(e),Matt Sorum–drums,Hollywood Roses(m),Brent Spiner-Data,Star Trek(w),Sting(t),Keisha Kerreece Fayeanne Brown Buchanan–Sugababes(w),Heidi India Range–Sugababes(m),Arsenium Todiraş–Ozone(m),Marisa Tomei(f),Faustin Archange Touadéra(w),Obie Trice(t),Alvaro Velez(m),Jimbo Jimmy Donald Wales(e),John Wayne(t),Rosemarie Wenner-sanctity(w),Shane West-Ray,ER(f), Alan White-drums,Oasis(m),Brad Whitford-guitar,Aerosmith(e),Sheree Julienne Wilson-April,Dallas(w),William Arthur Philip Louis Wales Windsor-majesty(t),Rachel Claire Ward – Meggie, The Thorn Birds (f), Boris Nikolayevich Yeltsin (f), Vicki Wei Zhao (w)

The transposition, shifted with 15 degrees, of the Chinese zodiac, over the classical one and the link with the reality of our times:

The Chinese pillar of the month: the Chinese month of the rabbit contains in the middle of it the spring equinox (21 March).The classical zodiac: the first sign, the Aries, starts with the spring equinox (vernal).The first zodiacal degree, 0, of the Aries is on 21 March, the degree 15 is on 5 April, when the dragon Chinese month begins.

Conclusion: Any Chinese month, by extension, <u>any Chinese sign begins with the degree 15 and ends in the next classical sign at the degree 14.</u>

Knowing this,with calculi or from the ephemeredes tables(described also at the chapter of the classical zodiac)we can find our signs,which correspond mostly to our Solar system :

- <u>the Chinese zodiacal sign of the *Sun*,</u> so by what degrees, of the circle that surrounds the Earth, passes the Sun, this corresponds to the Chinese month's pillar:

star	Roman deities	Greek deities
Sun	Apolo,Adam,Andrew,Daniel,Hari,Christ,Mahomed Michael,Mihaela,John,Ştefania,An,Christ,Hercules Sorana,Soleiman,Sorin,Sorina,Salmoxis,Zoroastru	Cneph,Helios,Hrist,Bogdan,Dhana,Phoeibous,Rada,Radu,Andrew Heracles,Haludiel,Hrist,Hannah,Danielle,Chassiel,Corat,Burchat Suleiman,Ştefan,Zalmolxis,Salmolxes,Samolxe,Zalmolxe,Zaratustra

- <u>the Chinese animal of the Earth's satellite,the *Moon*</u>(not the Moon's Chinese zodiac):

satellite	Roman deities	Greek deities
Moon	Luna,Leto,Diana,Proserpine,Andrew,Andrea	Eve,Gabriel,Gabrielle,Artemis,Deianira,Selena,Persephone,Hecate

- <u>the Chinese animals of the *planets*</u>, that travel around the Sun. Usually the signs of all the satellites are generally associated with the sign of the planet that they surround, being close to their planet:

planets	Roman deities	Greek deities
Earth, Terra, Globe	Telure,Tara,Ceres,Rhea,Silvania,Christos,Dochia	Demetra,Dumitru,Daniela,Dan,Cibele,Hristos,Tera,Gaea,Gaia
Mercury	Mercury,Maria,Mahdia,Mahdi,Messiah,Hrist	Christ,Christiana,Baraborat,Hermes,Raphaël,Moses,Mohamed
Venus	Venus,Uriel,Murcia,Mirtea,Maria,Bogdana,Eve	Eva,Haya,Chaya,Chaba,Hagiel,Abd,Aminah,Afrodita,Aphrodite
Mars	Mars,Marcus,Marusia,Mark,Tyr,Khamael,Peter	Simon,Simona,Samael,George,Zamael,Draga,Dragoş,Ares
Jupiter	Jupiter,Junona,Joanne,John,Joachim,Zachariel,Jesus	Muhamad,Muhamadia,Hera,Zeus,Zea,Zsalmolxe,Salmolxis
Saturn	Saturn,Steven,Salmolxis,Orifiel,Tzaphiel,Mathew	Cassiel,George,Georgiana,Chronos,Ianos,Josephine,Joseph
Uranus	Uranus,Pourushasp,Cambiel,Terra,Thaddeus,Dan	Peter,Uriel,Urania,Uranus,Ouranus,Ourania,Oceanus,Thetis
Neptune	Neptune,Barchiel,Anamaria,Pontus,Maria,Nereus	Poseidon,Maria,Matthias,Jesus,Ana,Anne,Asariel,Amphitrita,Triton
Pluto	Pluto,Pluton,Phili,Orchus,Azrael,Azraela,Thomas	George,Pintea,Palas,Aita,Hades,Cerberus,Tatarus,Tartarus

- <u>the Chinese animals of the *points from the space*</u>: <u>the opposed nods of the Moon (south nod=descending nod=tail of the dragon=Ketu</u>, in Sanskrit and <u>north nod=ascension nod =head of the dragon=Rahu</u>, in Sanskrit, nods of the trajectory of the Moon); the <u>black Moon=Lilith</u>(the empty focus of the Moon's trajectory); of an imaginary planet named <u>Vulcan</u>(Roman deity Vulcan=Greek deity Hephaestus)which would be between Mercury and Sun; of the <u>luck point=fortune point</u>(one of some Arab points, also a point derived from the trajectory of the Moon)

- <u>the Chinese animals of the *asteroids*</u> (the biggest is <u>Chiron</u>, at Greeks the centaur):

asteroids	Roman deities	Greek deities
Ceres	Ceres,Cerealia,Consiva,Christos,Telure,Daniela	Cibele,Hristos,Tera,Geb,Gelu,Glad,Shudhodana,Demetra,Demeter
Athena	Ageleia,Minerva,Mira,Mera,Menumorut,Teana	Pallas Athena,Atlas,Agorae,Cidonia,Hipea,Doorga,Nike
Vesta	Vesta, Sacerdos Virgo Vestalis, Vestia	Maria,Mary,Maia,Martin,Hestia,Histia,Tabiti,Dughdhava,Dello
Juno	Junona,Jupiter,Uni,Domiduca,Luke,Lucina	Hera,Zeus,Chera,Antheia,Pais,Prodrom,Basileia
Hygeia	Salus,Salutare,Sanitas,Ave,Valetudo	Ugeia,Hugieia,Hygeia,Hygienia,Igea,Jaso

- <u>the Chinese animals of the *ascendant* and of the other *cusps*</u> of the classical zodiac

Because this Chinese zodiac transposed on the classical one, was not made by the Chinese (not having the technical means to find all the celestial bigger bodies and their ways with the exactness of our days, so their trajectories transposed on the circle of the zodiacal degrees; this <u>circle of the zodiac signs</u> = <u>the ecliptic</u>, is slicing the entire Universe in two parts) by overlapping the Chinese signs upon the classical ones, we can find only the Chinese animal, but not also the element, because no one has made yet this zodiac, not existing a start for the cycle of the 60 binomials.

The deciphering of the Chinese zodiac and the link between it and the classical one is given by:

- planet Jupiter, which rotates itself once around the Sun, according to the calculations from thousands of years ago of the Chinese, in approximately 12 years (in the ephemeredes tables are calculated the exact degrees thru which passes Jupiter), gives the cycle of the 12 Chinese animals. This planet is the biggest in the solar system, visible from Earth and it was observed by many civilizations.

- planet Saturn, that gives the ideal zodiacal compatibilities of the Chinese elements, 2 rotations of approximately 30 years around the Sun, making the Chinese cycle of 60 years, by extension the cycles of the Chinese pillars

- the mathematical calculus that gives the cycle of the 60 binomials (the 60 divisions of time). The binomials are given by the 12 animals (1 Chinese hour or animal represents 2 hours), multiplied by the 5 elements, which represent the 5 planets(plainers visible on the sky) known at that time: Mercury, Venus, Mars, Jupiter and Venus. Also after 10 binomials, the same cycle of the elements follows, one element covering two animals, giving a yang binomial(the Sun) and a yin one(the Moon); once, the Chinese week was of 10 days (the decan).

The biblical sevennight(7 hebdomadal;west,north,up,center,down,south,east; head,neck,trunk,members; points of the lady buburuza bird bug beetle coccinellidae martin majesty maria; anemone trientalis)week:

French	lundi	mardi	mercredi	jeudi	vendredi	samedi	dimanche
Romanian	luni	marți	miercuri	joi	vineri	sâmbătă	duminică
Roman deities	Luna	Mars	Mercury	Jupiter	Venus	Saturn	Sun
German deities	Moon	Tyr	Wodan	Thor	Frigga		
English	Monday	Tuesday	Wednesday	Thursday	Friday	Saturday	Sunday
Vedic deities Sanscrits	Shiva	Subramanya	Vishnu	Indra	Indrani	Shani	Surya
	indu-va.	bhomya-vasara	chrisna-va.	brihaspativ.	barghava.	sthirava.	ravivar
	soma-v.	mangal-var	budha-var	jeeva-var	sukra-var	shani-v.	adivar
Japanese deities Japanese	Tsuki	KaSei	SuiSei	MokuSei	KinSei	DouSei	Taiyou
	getsu y.	ka youbi	sui youbi	moku y.	kin youbi	dou y.	nichi y.
in Hebraic	y. shinon	yom shlishi	yom revi'i	y. chamishi	y. shishi	shabbat	y. rishon
Portuguese	segunda f.	terca feira	quarta feira	quinta fe.	sexta fe.	sabado	domingo
Arabic are numbers	2	3	4	5	6	7	1
pharaohs	3	4	5	6	7	1	2
Slavic, Greek, Chinese	1	2	3	4	5	6	7

7 biblical skies or months of gravidity and amenorrhea with the baby after 2 months of amenorrhea with gravidity, 40 x 7 = 4 x 10 x 7 = 4 x 70 = 28 x 10 = 280 days = 9 months

The Chinese zodiac of the Moon:

The pillar of the Moon's Chinese year: There is the Sun's Chinese zodiac, the described one, but there is also a Chinese zodiac of the Moon, when the Moon's Chinese year begins in different days from January or February, in function of the same type of the Moon's fazes seen on the sky in a solar year, that depend of the Moon's cycle of rotations around the Earth (one rotation = one lunation = a Chinese month of the Moon = 29.5 days). The solar year (the cycle of the seasons and the night and day cycle) contains approximately between 12 and 13 months of the Moon. The Chinese years of the Moon, in order to begin always in January or February, so close to II 4, contain when 12, when 13 Chinese months of the Moon, consequently, more variants appear.

The pillar of the Moon's Chinese month begins at other dates and hours.

The pillars of the Moon's Chinese day and hour are not changed.

But if only 12 Chinese months of the Moon are always taken, then the Moon's year will begin at anytime in the solar year. The computer programs with the four Moon's pillars are lacking because of the multiple methods.

The Boreal Austral Zodiac
and the Mathematical Relation with the Chinese Zodiac

This zodiac is a Japanese classification of the 60 Chinese binomials, a Chinese binomial (a Chinese element + a Chinese animal) becoming a Boreal Austral animal. The Nippon animals are also all over the world, and represent means of increasing the equity and decreasing the inequity.

Examples:

rooster t(Chinese binomial 22)=pegasus powerfully winged

snake w(Chinese binomial 30)=wolf who adapts himself easily

Boreal Austral animal	Tree	Metal	tree	metal
cheetah	1. rat long distance runner	7. horse who sprints	42. snake robust	48. pig full of distinction
fawn	11. dog honest	17. dragon making proof of will	32. sheep making proof of courage	38. buffalo glamorous
pegasus	21. monkey calm	27. tiger with a moving life	22. rooster powerfully winged	28. rabbit elegant
elephant	31. horse leader	37. rat who drills	12. pig who wants to be popular	18. snake delicate
castor	41. dragon to whom the talents are flowering a bit later	47. dog humanist	2. buffalo who loves the mundanities	8. sheep civilized
lion	51. tiger making proof of autonomy	57. monkey full of emotions	52. rabbit leader	58. rooster fragile

43

Fire	Water	Earth	fire	water	earth	Boreal Austral animal
43. horse **agitated**	49. rat **making proof of serenity**	55. horse **full of power**	54. snake **who positivates**	60. pig **making proof of charity**	6. snake **loving**	**tiger**
33. monkey **full of action**	39. tiger **very romantic**	45. monkey **welcoming**	4. rabbit **agitated**	10. rooster **very maternal**	16. rabbit **typical**	**koala**
23. dog **making proof of naivety**	29. dragon **who launches to herself provocations**	35. dog **who needs the trust of the others**	14. buffalo **unadapted to the society**	20. sheep **quiet**	26.buffalo **making proof of tenacity**	**sheep**
13. rat **full of joy**	19. horse **going without a purpose**	25. rat **making proof of gentility**	24. pig **creative**	30. snake **who adapts himself easily**	36. pig **full of sympathy**	**wolf**
3. tiger **full of dynamism**	9. monkey **full of ambition**	15. tiger **making proof of determination**	34. rooster **full of fantasy**	40. rabbit **full of devotion**	46. rooster **who protects herself**	**monkey**
53. dragon **sentimental**	59. dog **making proof of independence**	5. dragon **who likes to return services**	44. sheep **full of passion**	50. buffalo **who depresses**	56. sheep **full of modesty**	**panther**

www.axatv.ro
www.bestmusic.ro
www.catmusic.ro
www.cinematograph.ro
www.dordetara.com
www.e-muzica.net
www.fermademuzica.ro
www.folclor.info
www.folcloric.ro
www.mandy.com
www.music.com
www.musicarena.ro
www.musicmall.ro
www.musicmix.ro
www.muzica.md
www.muzica.ro
www.muzicabuna.ro
www.myband.ro
www.pamparam.md
www.tvsighet.ro

The Fengshui,feng(wind) shui(water)=the celestial cervical energy or horse steam power (y=i=gi=ji=zi=li=qi=ki=ci=chi=hi=ti=di=si=mi=ri)of the 9 stars(7 from the Grate Chariot, the members, the abdomen, the thorax, the neck with the cervical vertebrae or 2 ears,2 nostrils,2 digestive orifices,1 excretory orifice;the Vega star and the Polar star, the mandible and the cranium or the 2 eyes)=Ki Ga Ku=Qi Gong=ReiKi=the biblical energy from paradise,eden,heaven,sky,cosmos=RaiChi, appeared in China and was developed in Japan and in other countries.There are 9 fengshui numbers(named also with a color and an element). Here also there are 4 pillars(hour, day, month, year). These are given by the succession of the 9 numbers(9 months of pregnancy),according to each pillar,from 9 to 1 (9, 8, 7, 6, 5, 4, 3, 2, 1, 9, 8, ...) or from 1 to 9 (1, 2, 3, 4, 5, 6, 7, 8, 9, 1, 2, 3, ...).

There are different systems of calculus:

-a system that uses one calculus: the rubrics from the woman or the ones from the man

-a system with two calculi: one for the woman (4 fengshui pillars) and another for the man (other 4 fengshui pillars), so two different fengshui cycles. An unclear thing remains when we make the calculus of the calendar date, in general, not of a person, because we don't know what gender to give to this date or at the previsions for a person when we compare calendar dates with the birth date of that person.

The fengshui square represents the shell of a turtle with the head at south (not from 1 to 9 or 9 to 1, but according to the cardinal points):

North-West	North	North-East
2 **EARTH** black	**1** **WATER** white	**4** **TREE** green
7 West **METAL** red	**5** center **EARTH** yellow	**3** East **TREE** turquoise
6 **METAL** white South-West	**9** **FIRE** red South	**8** **EARTH** white South-East

The calculation of the 4 fengshui pillars of a person can be dun using the two tables with the mathematical dependence between:
- the month's fengshui pillar and the year's fengshui pillar
- the hour's fengshui pillar and the day's fengshui pillar
To use these tables we have to know, at first, the fengshui year and day.
Another modality is the day with day, hour with hour, month with month and year with year notation of the fengshui numbers, from the beginning of the zodiac.

The Chinese year pillar and the fengshui year pillar:

Knowing the type of the Chinese years' cycle, we find the fengshui year's number			
The type of Chinese cycle (I, II, III)	The standard period and the according binomial of the **solar Chinese year**	The number of the **fengshui year** of birth at the **woman**	The number of the **fengshui year** of birth at the **man**
II The 77th Chinese cycle, from the 26th great cycle of the Chinese years	II-4-1924 => II-3-1925 (binomial 1, rat Tree)	2	4
	II-4-1925 => II-3-1926 (binomial 2, buffalo tree)	3	3
	II-4-1926 => II-3-1927 (binomial 3, tiger Fire)	4	2
	II-4-1927 => II-3-1928 (binomial 4, rabbit fire)	5	1
	II-4-1928 => II-3-1929 (binomial 5, dragon Earth)	6	9
	II-4-1929 => II-3-1930 (binomial 6, snake earth)	7	8
	II-4-1930 => II-3-1931 (binomial 7, horse Metal)	8	7
	II-4-1931 => II-3-1932 (binomial 8, sheep metal)	9	6
	II-4-1932 => II-3-1933 (binomial 9, monkey Water)	1	5
	II-4-1933 => II-3-1934 (binomial 10, rooster water)	2	4
	II-4-1934 => II-3-1935 (binomial 11, dog Tree)	3	3
	II-4-1935 => II-3-1936 (binomial 12, pig tree)	4	2
	II-4-1936 => II-3-1937 (binomial 13, rat Fire)	5	1
	II-4-1937 => II-3-1938 (binomial 14, buffalo fire)	6	9
	II-4-1938 => II-3-1939 (binomial 15, tiger Earth)	7	8
	II-4-1939 => II-3-1940 (binomial 16, rabbit earth)	8	7
	II-4-1940 => II-3-1941 (binomial 17, dragon Metal)	9	6
	II-4-1941 => II-3-1942 (binomial 18, snake metal)	1	5
	II-4-1942 => II-3-1943 (binomial 19, horse Water)	2	4
	II-4-1943 => II-3-1944 (binomial 20, sheep water)	3	3
	II-4-1944 => II-3-1945 (binomial 21, monkey Tree)	4	2
	II-4-1945 => II-3-1946 (binomial 22, rooster tree)	5	1
	II-4-1946 => II-3-1947 (binomial 23, dog Fire)	6	9
	II-4-1947 => II-3-1948 (binomial 24, pig fire)	7	8
	II-4-1948 => II-3-1949 (binomial 25, rat Earth)	8	7
	II-4-1949 => II-3-1950 (binomial 26, buffalo earth)	9	6
	II-4-1950 => II-3-1951 (binomial 27, tiger Metal)	1	5
	II-4-1951 => II-3-1952 (binomial 28, rabbit metal)	2	4
	II-4-1952 => II-3-1953 (binomial 29, dragon Water)	3	3
	II-4-1953 => II-3-1954 (binomial 30, snake water)	4	2
	II-4-1954 => II-3-1955 (binomial 31, horse Tree)	5	1
	II-4-1955 => II-3-1956 (binomial 32, sheep tree)	6	9
	II-4-1956 => II-3-1957 (binomial 33, monkey Fire)	7	8
	II-4-1957 => II-3-1958 (binomial 34, rooster fire)	8	7
	II-4-1958 => II-3-1959 (binomial 35, dog Earth)	9	6
	II-4-1959 => II-3-1960 (binomial 36, pig earth)	1	5
	II-4-1960 => II-3-1961 (binomial 37, rat Metal)	2	4
	II-4-1961 => II-3-1962 (binomial 38, buffalo metal)	3	3
	II-4-1962 => II-3-1963 (binomial 39, tiger Water)	4	2
	II-4-1963 => II-3-1964 (binomial 40, rabbit water)	5	1
	II-4-1964 => II-3-1965 (binomial 41, dragon Tree)	6	9

The type of Chinese cycle (I, II, III)	The standard period and the according **binomial of the solar Chinese year**	The number of the **fengshui year** of birth at the **woman**	The number of the **fengshui year** of birth at the **man**
	II-4-1965 => II-3-1966 (binomial 42, snake tree)	7	8
	II-4-1966 => II-3-1967 (binomial 43, horse Fire)	8	7
	II-4-1967 => II-3-1968 (binomial 44, sheep fire)	9	6
	II-4-1968 => II-3-1969 (binomial 45, monkey Earth)	1	5
	II-4-1969 => II-3-1970 (binomial 46, rooster earth)	2	4
	II-4-1970 => II-3-1971 (binomial 47, dog Metal)	3	3
	II-4-1971 => II-3-1972 (binomial 48, pig metal)	4	2
	II-4-1972 => II-3-1973 (binomial 49, rat Water)	5	1
	II-4-1973 => II-3-1974 (binomial 50, buffalo water)	6	9
	II-4-1974 => II-3-1975 (binomial 51, tiger Tree)	7	8
	II-4-1975 => II-3-1976 (binomial 52, rabbit tree)	8	7
	II-4-1976 => II-3-1977 (binomial 53, dragon Fire)	9	6
	II-4-1977 => II-3-1978 (binomial 54, snake fire)	1	5
	II-4-1978 => II-3-1979 (binomial 55, horse Earth)	2	4
	II-4-1979 => II-3-1980 (binomial 56, sheep earth)	3	3
	II-4-1980 => II-3-1981 (binomial 57, monkey Metal)	4	2
	II-4-1981 => II-3-1982 (binomial 58, rooster metal)	5	1
	II-4-1982 => II-3-1983 (binomial 59, dog Water)	6	9
	II-4-1983 => II-3-1984 (binomial 60, pig water)	7	8
III The 78th Chinese cycle, from the 26th great cycle of the Chinese years	II-4-1984 => II-3-1985 (binomial 1, rat Tree)	8	7
	II-4-1985 => II-3-1986 (binomial 2, buffalo tree)	9	6
	II-4-1986 => II-3-1987 (binomial 3, tiger Fire)	1	5
	II-4-1987 => II-3-1988 (binomial 4, rabbit fire)	2	4
	II-4-1988 => II-3-1989 (binomial 5, dragon Earth)	3	3
	II-4-1989 => II-3-1990 (binomial 6, snake earth)	4	2
	II-4-1990 => II-3-1991 (binomial 7, horse Metal)	5	1
	II-4-1991 => II-3-1992 (binomial 8, sheep metal)	6	9
	II-4-1992 => II-3-1993 (binomial 9, monkey Water)	7	8
	II-4-1993 => II-3-1994 (binomial 10, rooster water)	8	7
	II-4-1994 => II-3-1995 (binomial 11, dog Tree)	9	6
	II-4-1995 => II-3-1996 (binomial 12, pig tree)	1	5
	II-4-1996 => II-3-1997 (binomial 13, rat Fire)	2	4
	II-4-1997 => II-3-1998 (binomial 14, buffalo fire)	3	3
	II-4-1998 => II-3-1999 (binomial 15, tiger Earth)	4	2
	II-4-1999 => II-3-2000 (binomial 16, rabbit earth)	5	1
	II-4-2000 => II-3-2001 (binomial 17, dragon Metal)	6	9
	II-4-2001 => II-3-2002 (binomial 18, snake metal)	7	8
	II-4-2002 => II-3-2003 (binomial 19, horse Water)	8	7
	II-4-2003 => II-3-2004 (binomial 20, sheep water)	9	6
	II-4-2004 => II-3-2005 (binomial 21, monkey Tree)	1	5
	II-4-2005 => II-3-2006 (binomial 22, rooster tree)	2	4
	II-4-2006 => II-3-2007 (binomial 23, dog Fire)	3	3
	II-4-2007 => II-3-2008 (binomial 24, pig fire)	4	2

The type of Chinese cycle (I, II, III)	The standard period and the according **binomial of the solar Chinese year**	The number of the **fengshui year** of birth at the **woman**	The number of the **fengshui year** of birth at the **man**
	II-4-2008 => II-3-2009 (binomial 25, rat Earth)	5	1
	II-4-2009 => II-3-2010 (binomial 26, buffalo earth)	6	9
	II-4-2010 => II-3-2011 (binomial 27, tiger Metal)	7	8
	II-4-2011 => II-3-2012 (binomial 28, rabbit metal)	8	7
	II-4-2012 => II-3-2013 (binomial 29, dragon Water)	9	6
	II-4-2013 => II-3-2014 (binomial 30, snake water)	1	5
	II-4-2014 => II-3-2015 (binomial 31, horse Tree)	2	4
	II-4-2015 => II-3-2016 (binomial 32, sheep tree)	3	3
	II-4-2016 => II-3-2017 (binomial 33, monkey Fire)	4	2
	II-4-2017 => II-3-2018 (binomial 34, rooster fire)	5	1
	II-4-2018 => II-3-2019 (binomial 35, dog Earth)	6	9
	II-4-2019 => II-3-2020 (binomial 36, pig earth)	7	8
	II-4-2020 => II-3-2021 (binomial 37, rat Metal)	8	7
	II-4-2021 => II-3-2022 (binomial 38, buffalo metal)	9	6
	II-4-2022 => II-3-2023 (binomial 39, tiger Water)	1	5
	II-4-2023 => II-3-2024 (binomial 40, rabbit water)	2	4
	II-4-2024 => II-3-2025 (binomial 41, dragon Tree)	3	3
	II-4-2025 => II-3-2026 (binomial 42, snake tree)	4	2
	II-4-2026 => II-3-2027 (binomial 43, horse Fire)	5	1
	II-4-2027 => II-3-2028 (binomial 44, sheep fire)	6	9
	II-4-2028 => II-3-2029 (binomial 45, monkey Earth)	7	8
	II-4-2029 => II-3-2030 (binomial 46, rooster earth)	8	7
	II-4-2020 => II-3-2031 (binomial 47, dog Metal)	9	6
	II-4-2031 => II-3-2032 (binomial 48, pig metal)	1	5
	II-4-2032 => II-3-2033 (binomial 49, rat Water)	2	4
	II-4-2033 => II-3-2034 (binomial 50, buffalo water)	3	3
	II-4-2034 => II-3-2035 (binomial 51, tiger Tree)	4	2
	II-4-2035 => II-3-2036 (binomial 52, rabbit tree)	5	1
	II-4-2036 => II-3-2037 (binomial 53, dragon Fire)	6	9
	II-4-2037 => II-3-2038 (binomial 54, snake fire)	7	8
	II-4-2038 => II-3-2039 (binomial 55, horse Earth)	8	7
	II-4-2039 => II-3-2040 (binomial 56, sheep earth)	9	6
	II-4-2040 => II-3-2041 (binomial 57, monkey Metal)	1	5
	II-4-2041 => II-3-2042 (binomial 58, rooster metal)	2	4
	II-4-2042 => II-3-2043 (binomial 59, dog Water)	3	3
	II-4-2043 => II-3-2044 (binomial 60, pig water)	4	2
I The 79th Chinese cycle, from the 27th great cycle of the Chinese years	II-4-2044 => II-3-2045 (binomial 1, rat Tree)	5	1
	II-4-2045 => II-3-2046 (binomial 2, buffalo tree)	6	9
	II-4-2046 => II-3-2047 (binomial 3, tiger Fire)	7	8
	II-4-2047 => II-3-2048 (binomial 4, rabbit fire)	8	7
	II-4-2048 => II-3-2049 (binomial 5, dragon Earth)	9	6
	II-4-2049 => II-3-2050 (binomial 6, snake earth)	1	5
	II-4-2050 => II-3-2051 (binomial 7, horse Metal)	2	4

The type of Chinese cycle (I, II, III)	The standard period and the according **binomial of the solar Chinese year**	The number of the **fengshui year** of birth at the **woman**	The number of the **fengshui year** of birth at the **man**
	II-4-2051 => II-3-2052 (binomial 8, sheep metal)	3	3
	II-4-2052 => II-3-2053 (binomial 9, monkey Water)	4	2
	II-4-2053 => II-3-2054 (binomial 10, rooster water)	5	1
	II-4-2054 => II-3-2055 (binomial 11, dog Tree)	6	9
	II-4-2055 => II-3-2056 (binomial 12, pig tree)	7	8
	II-4-2056 => II-3-2057 (binomial 13, rat Fire)	8	7
	II-4-2057 => II-3-2058 (binomial 14, buffalo fire)	9	6
	II-4-2058 => II-3-2059 (binomial 15, tiger Earth)	1	5
	II-4-2059 => II-3-2060 (binomial 16, rabbit earth)	2	4
	II-4-2060 => II-3-2061 (binomial 17, dragon Metal)	3	3
	II-4-2061 => II-3-2062 (binomial 18, snake metal)	4	2
	II-4-2062 => II-3-2063 (binomial 19, horse Water)	5	1
	II-4-2063 => II-3-2064 (binomial 20, sheep water)	6	9
	II-4-2064 => II-3-2065 (binomial 21, monkey Tree)	7	8
	II-4-2065 => II-3-2066 (binomial 22, rooster tree)	8	7
	II-4-2066 => II-3-2067 (binomial 23, dog Fire)	9	6
	II-4-2067 => II-3-2068 (binomial 24, pig fire)	1	5
	II-4-2068 => II-3-2069 (binomial 25, rat Earth)	2	4
	II-4-2069 => II-3-2070 (binomial 26, buffalo earth)	3	3
	II-4-2070 => II-3-2071 (binomial 27, tiger Metal)	4	2
	II-4-2071 => II-3-2072 (binomial 28, rabbit metal)	5	1
	II-4-2072 => II-3-2073 (binomial 29, dragon Water)	6	9
	II-4-2073 => II-3-2074 (binomial 30, snake water)	7	8
	II-4-2074 => II-3-2075 (binomial 31, horse Tree)	8	7
	II-4-2075 => II-3-2076 (binomial 32, sheep tree)	9	6
	II-4-2076 => II-3-2077 (binomial 33, monkey Fire)	1	5
	II-4-2077 => II-3-2078 (binomial 34, rooster fire)	2	4
	II-4-2078 => II-3-2079 (binomial 35, dog Earth)	3	3
	II-4-2079 => II-3-2080 (binomial 36, pig earth)	4	2
	II-4-2080 => II-3-2081 (binomial 37, rat Metal)	5	1
	II-4-2081 => II-3-2082 (binomial 38, buffalo metal)	6	9
	II-4-2082 => II-3-2083 (binomial 39, tiger Water)	7	8
	II-4-2083 => II-3-2084 (binomial 40, rabbit water)	8	7
	II-4-2084 => II-3-2085 (binomial 41, dragon Tree)	9	6
	II-4-2085 => II-3-2086 (binomial 42, snake tree)	1	5
	II-4-2086 => II-3-2087 (binomial 43, horse Fire)	2	4
	II-4-2087 => II-3-2088 (binomial 44, sheep fire)	3	3
	II-4-2088 => II-3-2089 (binomial 45, monkey Earth)	4	2
	II-4-2089 => II-3-2090 (binomial 46, rooster earth)	5	1
	II-4-2090 => II-3-2091 (binomial 47, dog Metal)	6	9
	II-4-2091 => II-3-2092 (binomial 48, pig metal)	7	8
	II-4-2092 => II-3-2093 (binomial 49, rat Water)	8	7
	II-4-2093 => II-3-2094 (binomial 50, buffalo water)	9	6

The type of Chinese cycle (I, II, III)	The standard period and the according **binomial of the solar Chinese year**	The number of the **fengshui year** of birth at the **woman**	The number of the **fengshui year** of birth at the **man**
	II-4-2094 => II-3-2095 (binomial 51, tiger Tree)	1	5
	II-4-2095 => II-3-2096 (binomial 52, rabbit tree)	2	4
	II-4-2096 => II-3-2097 (binomial 53, dragon Fire)	3	3
	II-4-2097 => II-3-2098 (binomial 54, snake fire)	4	2
	II-4-2098 => II-3-2099 (binomial 55, horse Earth)	5	1
	II-4-2099 => II-3-2100 (binomial 56, sheep earth)	6	9
	II-4-2100 => II-3-2101 (binomial 57, monkey Metal)	7	8
	II-4-2101 => II-3-2102 (binomial 58, rooster metal)	8	7
	II-4-2102 => II-3-2103 (binomial 59, dog Water)	9	6
	II-4-2103 => II-3-2104 (binomial 60, pig water)	1	5
II The 80th Chinese cycle, from the 27th great cycle of the Chinese years	II-4-2104 => II-3-2105 (binomial 1, rat Tree)	2	4
	II-4-2105 => II-3-2106 (binomial 2, buffalo tree)	3	3
	II-4-2106 => II-3-2107 (binomial 3, tiger Fire)	4	2
	II-4-2107 => II-3-2108 (binomial 4, rabbit fire)	5	1
	II-4-2108 => II-3-2109 (binomial 5, dragon Earth)	6	9
	II-4-2109 => II-3-2110 (binomial 6, snake earth)	7	8
	II-4-2110 => II-3-2111 (binomial 7, horse Metal)	8	7

We see in the table that the fengshui numbers are repeating themselves in the same way after 3 Chinese cycles, so after a great cycle (180 Chinese binomials). This is the link between fengshui and the Chinese zodiac. Each cycle (I, II, III) has the binomials in a specific different order. Thus, the 77th Chinese cycle, a cycle II, from the 26th great Chinese cycle has the same fengshui numbers, for the same Chinese binomials, with the 80th Chinese cycle, also a cycle II, from the 27th great Chinese cycle, so with any cycle II.

The daylight saving time (exemplified at the Chinese zodiac) can modify the fengshui numbers (someone born in may 5 1987 at the hour 00:20 at night, but in the daylight saving time of an hour, has also the Chinese and fengshui standard hour 23:20, so we calculate the Chinese and fengshui pillars for the standard date and hour: may 4 1987, 23:20). After that, if we use the method of the meridian from Beiging or from any other locality, the same thing can happen with the standard hour or date.

http://sighetumarmatiei.alphanet.ro
http://www.memorialsighet.ro
http://www.wikipedia.org/wiki/Category:Monuments_and_memorials
http://en.wikipedia.org/wiki/Category:Aromanians
www.en.wikipedia.org/wiki/Category:Bilateral_relations_of_Romania
www.en.wikipedia.org/wiki/Category:Book_publishing_companies_of_Romania
www.en.wikipedia.org/wiki/Category:Categories_by_country
www.en.wikipedia.org/wiki/Category:Media_by_country
www.en.wikipedia.org/wiki/Category:Romanian_literature
www.en.wikipedia.org/wiki/Category:Romanian_media
www.en.wikipedia.org/wiki/Category:Romanian_music
www.en.wikipedia.org/wiki/Category:Romanian_people_by_occupation
www.en.wikipedia.org/wiki/Category:Romanian_television
www.en.wikipedia.org/wiki/Romanian_educational_system
www.ro.wikipedia.org/wiki/Categorie:Cinematografie
www.ro.wikipedia.org/wiki/Categorie:Teatre

The fengshui year can be found at:
www.chineseastrologyonline.com/fsdir.htm

The link between the great cycle of the Chinese years and the fengshui years (a great cycle being of 180 Chinese binomials = 3 Chinese cycles (I,II,III) each of 60 Chinese binomials) is also here:

The mathematical link between the **Chinese year** and the **fengshui** year(shown in the precedent table too)									
The number of the **fengshui year** of birth at the **woman**	7	6	5	4	3	2	1	9	8
The number of the **fengshui year** of birth at the **man**	8	9	1	2	3	4	5	6	7
I Chinese cycle	3	2	1						
	12	11	10	9	8	7	6	5	4
	21	20	19	18	17	16	15	14	13
	30	29	28	27	25	25	24	23	22
	39	38	37	36	35	34	33	32	31
	48	47	46	45	44	43	42	41	40
	57	56	55	54	53	52	51	50	49
II Chinese cycle	6	5	4	3	2	1			
	15	14	13	12	11	10	9	8	7
	24	23	22	21	20	19	18	17	16
	33	32	31	30	29	28	27	26	25
	42	41	40	39	38	37	36	35	34
	51	50	49	48	47	46	45	44	43
	60	59	58	57	56	55	54	53	52
III Chinese cycle	9	8	7	6	5	4	3	2	1
	18	17	16	15	14	13	12	11	10
	27	26	25	24	23	22	21	20	19
	36	35	34	33	32	31	30	29	28
	45	44	43	42	41	40	39	38	37
	54	53	52	51	50	49	48	47	46
				60	59	58	57	56	55
I It can be seen that the distribution of the fengshui numbers over the Chinese binomials, is repeating itself like at I	3	2	1						
	12	11	10	9	8	7	6	5	4
	21	20	19	18	17	16	15	14	13
	30	29	28	27	25	25	24	23	22
	39	38	37	36	35	34	33	32	31

Knowing the fengshui year pillar, we find the fengshui month pillar:

Woman			
Standard period	The fengshui **year**		
	1, 4, 7	3, 6, 9	5, 2, 8
II 4 - III 5	7	1	4
III 6 - IV 4	8	2	5
IV 5 - V 5	9	3	6
V 6 - VI 5	1	4	7
VI 6 - VII 7	2	5	8
VII 8 - VIII 7	3	6	9
VIII 8 - IX 7	4	7	1
IX 8 - X 8	5	8	2
X 9 - XI 7	6	9	3
XI 8 - XII 6	7	1	4
XII 7 - I 5	8	2	5
I 6 - II 3	9	3	6
	The fengshui **month**		

Man			
Standard period	The fengshui **year**		
	1, 4, 7	3, 6, 9	5, 2, 8
II 4 - III 5	8	5	2
III 6 - IV 4	7	4	1
IV 5 - V 5	6	3	9
V 6 - VI 5	5	2	8
VI 6 - VII 7	4	1	7
VII 8 - VIII 7	3	9	6
VIII 8 - IX 7	2	8	5
IX 8 - X 8	1	7	4
X 9 - XI 7	9	6	3
XI 8 - XII 6	8	5	2
XII 7 - I 5	7	4	1
I 6 - II 3	6	3	9
	The fengshui **month**		

The fengshui day has multiple calculi with different results that can be found from the internet, the row of the numbers being increasingly, decreasingly, or alternatively, consequently also the fengshui hour; the link between these two is:

Woman			
Standard hour	The fengshui **day**		
	1, 4, 7	3, 6, 9	5, 2, 8
24-1	5	2	8
1-3	4	1	7
3-5	3	9	6
5-7	2	8	5
7-9	1	7	4
9-11	9	6	3
11-13	8	5	2
13-15	7	4	1
15-17	6	3	9
17-19	5	2	8
19-21	4	1	7
21-23	3	9	6
23-24	2	8	5
	The fengshui **hour**		

Man			
Standard hour	The fengshui **day**		
	1, 4, 7	3, 6, 9	5, 2, 8
24-1	1	4	7
1-3	2	5	8
3-5	3	6	9
5-7	4	7	1
7-9	5	8	2
9-11	6	9	3
11-13	7	1	4
13-15	8	2	5
15-17	9	3	6
17-19	1	4	7
19-21	2	5	8
21-23	3	6	9
23-24	4	7	1
	The fengshui **hour**		

The fengshui pillars of the standard year, month and day, for some current dates, can be found at:
www.chineseastrologyonline.com/PWdaily.htm

The fengshui pillar of the standard hour, for some current dates, can be found at:
www.chineseastrologyonline.com/PWHours.htm

53

Discussions:

From some people's calculi we see that the fengshui day would begin at 23, at the same time with the fengshui hour's pillar 23-1(the standard hours of the clock).

1 fengshui hour = 1 Chinese hour = 2 hours of the clock

These are the same shifts encountered at the Chinese zodiac and at the other calendars:

- if the fengshui day begins:
- at the hour 23, with the fengshui hours:
23-1, 1-3, 3-5, 5-7,…, 21-23
- at the hour 00, with the fengshui hours:
00-1, 1-3, 3-5, 5-7,…, 21-23, 23-00
- at the hour 00, and then the fengshui hours to be from:
00-2, 2-4, 4-6, 6-8,…, 22-00

- if the fengshui solar year begins:
- at December 8 (with the first Chinese animal: the rat)
- in February 4 (with the Chinese month of the tiger)
- at January 1, at the same time with the Gregorian present day year, with the rat's or tiger's Chinese month

WATER(1) => TREE(3,4) => FIRE(9) => EARTH(2,5,8) => METAL(6,7) => WATER(1)						
Maximized monachism			**Maximized monachism**		**Maximized familism**	
woman	woman		man	man	woman	man
1	3; 4; 6; 7		1	3; 4; 6; 7	1	2; 5; 8
2	6; 7; 9		2	6; 7; 9	2; 5; 8	3; 4
3	1; 9		3	1; 9	3; 4	6; 7
4	1; 9		4	1; 9	6; 7	9
5	6; 7; 9		5	6; 7; 9	9	1
6	1; 2; 5; 8		6	1; 2; 5; 8		
7	1; 2; 5; 8		7	1; 2; 5; 8		
8	6; 7; 9		8	6; 7; 9		
9	2; 3; 4; 5; 8		9	2; 3; 4; 5; 8		

WATER(1) => FIRE(9) => METAL(6,7) => TREE(3,4) => EARTH(2,5,8) => WATER(1)						
Minimized monachism			Minimized monachism		Minimized familism	
woman	woman		man	man	woman	man
1	2; 5; 8; 9		1	2; 5; 8; 9	1	9
2	1; 3; 4		2	1; 3; 4	2; 5; 8	1
3	2; 5; 6; 7; 8		3	2; 5; 6; 7; 8	3; 4	2; 5; 8
4	2; 5; 6; 7; 8		4	2; 5; 6; 7; 8	6; 7	3; 4
5	1; 3; 4		5	1; 3; 4	9	6; 7
6	3; 4; 9		6	3; 4; 9		
7	3; 4; 9		7	3; 4; 9		
8	1; 3; 4		8	1; 3; 4		
9	1; 6; 7		9	1; 6; 7		

The Aztec Mayan Zodiac

Contains 20 zodiacal signs (the 20 digits: the fingers and the toes), that are days disposed on a big wheel (in the Aztec order: crocodile, wind, house, lizard, snake, death, deer, rabbit, water, dog, monkey, grass, reed, jaguar, eagle, vulture, earthquake, silex knife, rain, flower) and that are taken by the second smaller wheel with 13 indentations (3 major articulations x 4 members and the axis head articulation or the axonal cranial fascicles or the approximate 13 moons/solar year), 20 zodiacal signs x 13 numbers, give a cycle of 260 days, that is an Aztec year (as much as the gravity lasts at the woman, 243 days is the rotation of Venus around the Sun), each group of the 20 ones, of 13 numbers, has the name of the first zodiacal sign of the day and number 1 (trecena=13).

There is also the solar method where in an Aztec solar year there are 19 Aztec solar months, 18 of 20 days (18 x 20 = 360 days) and the 19th Aztec solar month is of 5 or 6 days (after an explained and established algorithm after the detection by the Aztecs of the shifting of the 365 days calendar with the solar seasons); the name of the solar Aztec months are different from the 20 zodiacal signs.

An Aztec century has 52 years (4 years x 13). A solar Aztec year can be only of 4 zodiac signs of the 20 ones: reed(east), silex knife(north), house(west) or rabbit(south), each animal passing 13 times thru the 52 years cycle.

In the 19th month of the Aztec solar years 1, 5, 9 of the rabbit, reed, silex knife and of the house are 6 days, in rest there are 5 days, with the exception of the house's year 13, where there are 6 days at 104, 208, 312, 416 years, and 5 days at 520 years (10 x 52 = 2 x 260 = 520).Thus it doesn't appear the shift between the Aztec solar years and the seasons.

Due to these different algorithms, our Gregorian calendar years do not coincide neither with the Aztec years of 260 days (=donalpohualli) and neither with the Aztec solar years of 365 or 366 days (=xiuhpohualli). At 52 years the two types of years coincide.

These numbers form also bigger periods (millenniums, eras).

There are also 9 nights.

Thus the day(=tonal) and the solar year(=xiuitl) have each:

  a zodiacal sign + a number (from 1 to 13)

The compatibilities exist between the animals and the numbers and are given by the parity, but the problem is given by the different methods of calculi and the date of the beginning of the calendar. In the Maya zodiac only the names and periods are sometimes different.

An interpretation is that we are each of the 20 zodiacal signs, or all the signs of the zodiacs.

The 20 Aztec Mayan Animals and the 4 elements of the classical zodiac			
E	water	♋ ♏ ♓	I, V, IX, XIII, XVII
N	air	♊ ♎ ♒	II, VI, X, XIV, XVIII
W	earth	♉ ♍ ♑	III, VII, XI, XV, XIX
S	fire	♈ ♌ ♐	IV, VIII, XII, XVI, XX

The 9 nights with the full Moon are the 9 months of pregnancy, 9 fengshui numbers, 9 biblical skies.

The 19 Aztec solar months	The 19 Mayan solar months	Deities by the 20 groups trecena	Deities by the 20 days	The 20 Aztec days and the Cardinal Points		The 20 Mayan days
Altacahualo (stopping of waters)	Pop (jaguar, mat)	Ometeotl Tonalcatecuhtli	Tonalcatecuhtli (nurturance, sustenance)	Cipactli (crocodile, caiman)	E	I.Imix, (waterlily, crocodile)
Tacaxipehualiztli (peeling, flaying)	Uo, Wo (frog)	Chantico (crater) Tezcatlipoca	Quetzalcoatl (feathered serpent)	Ehecatl (wind)	N	II.Ik, Iq (air, wind, life)
Tozoztontli (little vigil)	Zip, Sip (deer)	Itzpapalotl (butterfly with claws)	Tepeyollotl (heart of the mountain, jaguar)	Calli (house)	W	III.Akbal (night, subterranean)
Hueytozoztli (great vigil)	Zotz, Sots, Xoc (bat)	Itztlacoliuhqui Tezcatlipoca	Huehuecoyotl (archaic coyote)	Cuetzpalin (lizard)	S	IV.Kan, Kat (corn)
Txcatl (drought)	Tzecos, Sek (skull, sermon)	Xiuhtecuhtli (fire) Tlahuizcalpantecutli(dawn)	Chalchihuitlicue (waters)	Coatl, Cahuatl (serpent)	E	V.Chikchan, Kan (serpent)
Etzalcualiztli (eating maize and beans)	Xul (termination)	Tonatiuh (Sun)	Tecciztecatl (conch, Moon)	Miquiztli (immortality)	N	VI.Kimi, Kame (cranium, skull)
Tecuilhuitontli(small festivity of the deities)	Yax Kin (morning green Sun)	Tepeyollotl (heart of the mountain, jaguar)	Tlaloc (sprout, blossoming, rain, thunder, tsunami)	Mazatl (deer, stag)	W	VII.Manik, Kiej (deer)
Hueytecuilthuitli(great festivity of the deities)	Mol (reunion)	Xiuhtecuhtli (fire)	Mayahuel (maguey plant)	Tochtli (rabbit)	S	VIII.Lamat, Qanil (Venus, rabbit)
Tlaxochimaco(flowers) Miccailhuitontli (small festivity of immortality)	Chen (water well, Moon, black storm, the only one)	Chalchihuihtotolin (the jeweled fowl)	Xiuhtecuhtli (fire)	Atl (water)	E	IX.Muluc, Toj (Moon, rain, water)
Xocohuetzi (fruits) Hueymiccailhuitl (great festivity of immortality)	Yax (Venus, green storm hurricane typhoon, the first)	Xipe Totec (flaying, spring, rejuvenation)	Mictlantecuhtli (the immortality)	Itzcuintli (dog)	N	X.Tzi Ok (dog)
Ochpaniztli (sweeping)	Zac, Sak (white storm)	Patecatl (health)	Xochipili (flower)	Ozomatli (monkey)	W	XI.Chuwen, Batz (monkey, thread)
Pachtontli (small hay), Teotleco(returning)	Ceh, Keh (red storm)	Mayahuel (maguey plant, agaves)	Patecatl (health)	Malinalli (grass)	S	XII.Eb (broom, way, steers)
Hueipachtli (big hay), Tecpeihuitl (mountains)	Mac (cover)	Chalchihuitlicue (waters, river, lakes, seas, oceans)	Tezcatlipoca (smoking mirror, nocturnal sky)	Acatl (reed)	E	XIII.Ben, Aaj (green corn)
Quecholli (flamingo)	Kan Kin(the yellow Sun of the midday)	Quetzalcoatl (Venus rising, feathered serpent)	Tlazolteotl (Earth)	Ocelotl (jaguar)	N	XIV.Ix (jaguar)
Panquetzaliztli(raising of banners)	Moan, Muwan (owl, cloudy)	Xochiquetzal (flower feather, music, arts)	Xipe Totec (flaying, spring, rejuvenation)	Cuauhtl (eagle)	W	XV.Men, Tzikin (eagle, bird, hawk)
Atemoztli (the descent of water)	Pax (puma, jaguar, music)	Xolotl (double, Venus setting)	Itzpapalotl (butterfly with claws)	Cozcacuauhtli (condor, vulture)	S	XVI.Kib,Ajmaq(wax, knowledge, ancestors)
Titli (muscle stretching)	Kayab (great Moon, turtle)	Tlazolteotl (Earth)	Xolotl (double, Venus setting)	Ollin (seism)	E	XVII.Kaban, Noj (earthquake)
Izcalli (growth, rebirth)	Cumku (crocodile, granary)	Mictlantecuhtli (the immortality)	Chalchihuihtotolin (the jeweled fowl)	Tecpatl (silex knife)	N	XVIII.Etznab, Tijaax (flint)
Nementoni (the emptied days)	Uayeb (the emptied days)	Tlaloc (sprout, blossoming, rain, thunder, tsunami)	Tonatiuh (Sun)	Quiahuitl (rain)	W	XIX.Kawak (storm)
		Huehuecoyotl (archaic coyote)	Xochiquetzal (flower feather, music, arts)	Xochitl (flower)	S	XX.Ahau (chief, Sun)

Numbers at Maya and Aztecs			Birds	The Aztec and the classic constellations
1	Hun	Ce (Xiuhtecuhtli, fire)	Xiuhuitzilin (maroon hummingbird)	Itzpapalotl,The Butterfly with Claws (Dragon, Little Bear)
2	Ka	Ome (Tlaltecuhtli, Terra)	Quetzalhuitzilin (green hummingbird)	Malinalli, The Grass (Cepheus, Cassiopea)
3	Os,Ox	Yei (Chalchihuitlicue)	Huactli (falcon)	Xochitl, The Flower (Andromeda, Pegasus, Fishes, Aries)
4	Kan	Nahui (Tonatiuh, Sun)	Tecuzolin (quail)	Quetzalcoatl, Fethered Snake (Fishes,Wale,River,Phoenix)
5	Ho	Mahcuilli (Tlazolteotl)	Itzthotli (hawk)	Ollin, Earthquake (Great Lion, Small Lion)
6	Uak, Wak	Chicuacen (Michtlantecuhtli)	Chiquatli (cat-hollo scritch screech owl)	Tezcatlipoca, Smoked Mirror (Great Bear)
7	Uuk, Wuk	Chicome (Cinteotl, corn)	Papalotl (butterfly with claws)	Xonecuilli, The Blue Worm (Big Dog,Rabbit,River,Dove)
8	Uaxak, Wasac	Chicuei (Tlaloc,thunder)	Cuauhtli (eagle harpie vulture pajură gypaète gryphon zăgan)	Chalchiuhuitl, Emeralds (Small Dog, Hydre, Cancer)
9	Bolon, Bocon	Chicunahui (Quetzalcoatl)	Totolin (turkey)	Citlaltlachtli, The Game with the Mats (Gemini)
10	Lahun	Mahtlactli (Tezcatlipoca)	Tecolotl (hooter owl with tassels, tufts)	Tianquiztli, Market (Pleiades)
11	Buluc	Ma.-once(Chalmecatecuhtli)	Alo (scarlet macaw, red parrot)	Ozomatli, Monkey (Charioteer, Perseus)
12	Lahat	Ma.-omome (Tlalhuizcalpantecuhli)	Quetzaltotolin (quetzal, green parrot)	Colotlixayac, Scorpion Face (Taurus, Orion, Gemini)
13	Oxlahn	Ma.-omei (Ilamatecutli,stars)	Toznene (yellow parrot)	Mamalhuaztli, Torch (Orion)

The 9 nights								
Tiuztecuhli	Itztli(black)	Piltzintecuhtli(youth)	Cinteotl(corn)	Mictlantecuhtli	Chalchihuitlicue	Tlazolteotl	Tepeyolotl	Tlaloc

The Arab Zodiac of Agriculture

An Arab zodiac uses as zodiac signs 12 farming, medical, inflatable and constructing tools, utensils, instruments of 3 types: short (small knife, small dagger, big knife, big dagger), middle (mace, club, axe, chain) and long (sword, spear, sling, bow).

The zodiacal compatibilities are given by the correspondence of the significations											
January	February	Mars	April	May	June	July	August	September	October	November	December
Aquarius	Fishes	Aries	Taurus	Gemini	Cancer	Lion	Virgin	Libra	Scorpion	Sagittarius	Capricorn
Tiger	Rabbit	Dragon	Snake	Horse	Sheep	Monkey	Rooster	Dog	Pig	Rat	Buffalo
Sling, Ejection, Injection, Irrigation, Transpiration, Sweat, Pot, Can, Lactates, Milky, Whey, Well, Aquatic, Water, Fountain, Pomp, Source	Hatchet, Helm, Sale, Steer, Rudder, Liquefaction, Clarinet, Melt, Fluid, Floatable, Roots,Bulbs, Palette, Maul, Mall, Axe, Ax, Bardiche, Plow, Plough	Small Dacic Getic Dagger, Dredger, Direction, Dirk, Melon, Celt Skene, Creto-Greek Cresh, Criș, Roman Pugio, Martingale, Perforator, Screw, Screwdriver, Drill	Truncheon, Tractor, Traction, Harness, Pickaxe, Anchor, Hammer, Club, Cosh, Cudgel, Cylinder, Bulldozer, Bread,Arab Hebrew Mere,Pasta, Staff,Stick, Topuz	Bozdogan, Buzdugan, Crane, Steps, Scale, Gamut, Mace, Mallet, Mat, Balls, Balloon, Gag,Bit,Pumpkin, Marrow,Melon, Mane,Hair,Hairs, Colors, Claviers, Cinematography, Musical, Saw, Rake, Scepter	Big Knife, Plate, Deck, Insect, Arachnid, Keys, Wrench, Spanner, Scissors, Snips,Pincers, Pliers, Confections, Tongs, Nippers, Claws	Sword, Sabre, Saber, Katana,Tachi, Foil,Spoon, Scythe, Hoe, Spade, Big Yatagan, Rod,Mast, Link,Channel, Tail,Propeller, Ancestors, Relative, Stalk, Cord, Pale, Beam	Small Knife, Penknife,Little Spoon,Bistoury, Scalpel, Wheel, Screwdriver, Turndriver, Virtuosity,Nail, Vegetal, Wind, Whirlpool, Nut, Marabou, Bolt, Plain, Pecker, Aviation,Vigor, Latch, Sluice, Lock, Yale, Key	Chain, Leash, Lyre, Mouth,Muzzle, Bite, Necklace, Collar,Catena, Harness, Flail, Numchaks, Chinese Asiatic Nunchaku, Lever, Ghermăn, Scales, Balance	Big Arabian Dagger, Injection,Needle, Probe, Peg, Sickle, Allergen, Small Yatagan, Indian Tibetan Chinese Kukri,Excavator, Trumpet, Saxophone, Spider, Scissors,Snips, Tongs,Pliers, Criss, Criș, Claws	Bow, Arrow, Fiddle, Sled, Sleigh, Sledge, Troika, Syringe,Vaccine, Wind, Vault, Cupola, Roof, Geode, Rainbow, Seeds, Mill, Cascade, Barrage, Bridge,Passage, Saddle	Lance,Lancet, Spoon Large, Laddle, Masts, Stalk,Stiletto, Spanish Spear, Bugle, Siren, Flute, Cornet,Horn, Cactus,Harpoon, Javelin,Crane, Peg, Pitchfork, Dart,Darts,Fork, Cakes,Macaroni, Trocar, Sticks, Cannula,Spade, Needle,Rod, Nail, Pale

The calculation of the Arab zodiac sign is dun also with other tables of the 12 classical zodiac signs, the job of the parents and the number of inhabitants of the locality, the zodiac underlining the utilitarian biotechnological aspects of the science of the mechanization.

http://ddjag.free.fr/Fhorarab.htm   http://en.wikipedia.org/wiki/Category:Agriculture
http://es.wikipedia.org/wiki/Calendario_azteca   http://ro.wikipedia.org/wiki/Roxolani
http://pagesperso-orange.fr/atil/astro   http://ro.wikipedia.org/wiki/Categorie:Dacia
http://zodiac24.com www.sighet.go.ro www.mt.ro http://ro.wikipedia.org/wiki/Cumania
www.12zodii.ro   www.economia-online.ro/calculatoare-comunicatii/sighetu_marmatiei
www.acvaria.com www.web-top.ro/firme_pe_judet/Maramures/Sighetu_Marmatiei.html
www.americas-fr.com/calendrier/definitions.html   http://en.wikipedia.org/wiki/Solotvino
www.astrostar.com/AztecAstrology.htm   http://en.wikipedia.org/wiki/Marmatia
www.astrotheme.fr   www.economia-online.ro/divertisment-media/sighetu_marmatiei
www.aztec-astrology.com www.mcti.ro http://fr.wikipedia.org/wiki/Sighetu_Marmatiei
www.azteccalendar.com www.economia-online.ro/sanatate-frumusete/sighetu_marmatiei
www.astrodreamadvisor.com   http://residency-database.helmsic.gr   www.mmediu.ro
www.cienciaseternas.com   http://en.wikipedia.org/wiki/Category:Maramures
www.crystalinks.com/mayancalendar.html   http://ro.wikipedia.org/wiki/Sarmatia
www.dsclex.ro/astrolog/astrologie.htm www.economia-online.ro/auto/sighetu_marmatiei
www.horo.tv   www.madr.ro   www.economia-online.ro/agricultura/sighetu_marmatiei
www.horoscope.fr   www.economia-online.ro/turism-calatorii/sighetu_marmatiei
www.horoscoptv.ro   www.economia-online.ro/finante-juridic/sighetu_marmatiei
www.mayacalendar.com   www.economia-online.ro/educatie/sighetu_marmatiei
www.mayantimes.com/convertdatesimprved.htm   http://fr.wikipedia.org/wiki/Marmatie
www.mayasautenticos.com   www.economia-online.ro/constructii/sighetu_marmatiei
www.oroscopi.com www.mts.ro www.listafirme.ro/maramures/sighetu-marmatiei/o1.htm
www.pauahtun.org/Calendar/tools.html   http://en.wikipedia.org/wiki/Sighetu_Marmatiei
www.tortuga.com   www.economia-online.ro/constructii/mobila/sighetu_marmatiei
www.wikipedia.org/wiki/Calendar www.economia-online.ro/industrie/sighetu_marmatiei
www.zodiace.ro   www.afacerisighetene.ro   www.wikipedia.org/wiki/Category:Romania

The Classical Zodiac

Signification	Sanskrit	Sumerian	Coptic	Syrian	Hebrew	Arabic	Turkish	Greek	Latin
lamb,ewe,sheep,ram	Mesha	Luhunga	Tametouris	Amroo	Taleh	Hamal	Koc	Krios	Aries
calf,heifer,cow,ox,bull.	Vrishabha	Guda., Mul	Isis	Al Thaur	Shur	Thaur	Boga	Tauros	Taurus
twins	Mithuna	Mastabagal.	Pi Mahi	Thaumin	Thaumim	Tauman	Ikizler	Didumoi	Gemini
lobster,crab,cancer	Karka	Nangar	Klaria	Sartano	Sartan	Sartan	Yengec	Karkinos	Cancer
lionet,lioness,lion	Simha	Urgula,Latarak	Pi Mentekeon	Aryo	Arieh	Al Asad	Aslan	Leon	Leo
candid,virgin	Kanya	Absin,Shala	Aspolia	Bethulo	Bethulah	Sunbula	Basak	Parthenos	Virgo
balance,scales	Tula	Zibanitum,Utu	Lambadia	Mazatho	Mozanaim	Zubena	Terazi	Zygos	Libra
scorpion, arachnid	Vrishchika	Girtab,Ishhara	Isidis	Al Akrab	Akrab	Akrab	Akrep	Scorpios	Scorpio
bow,centaur,sag.	Dhanu	Papilsag	Pi Maere	Kisith	Kesith	Al Kaus	Yay	Toxotes	Sagitt.
kid,goat,buck,capr.	Makara	Suhur	Aigokereus	Hupenius	Gedi	Al Gedi	Oglak	Capricornus	Capric.
urn,water spiller	Kumbha	Gu, Gula	Hupei Tirion	Delu	Deli	Delu	Kova	Hydrokoeus	Aquarius
two fish	Mina	Zib,Iku,Nunu	Picot Orion	Nuno	Dagim	Al Haut	Balik	Ichthues	Pisces

http://philologos.org/__eb-mazzaroth

Maximized monachism			Minimized monachism	
Aries(Dragon)III	Lion(Monkey)VII	Sagittarius (Rat) XI	III (Dragon) Aries	Libra (Dog) IX
Taurus(Snake)IV	Virgin(Rooster)VIII	Capricorn(Buffalo)XII	IV (Snake) Taurus	Scorpion (Pig) X
Gemini(Horse)V	Libra (Dog) IX	Aquarius (Tiger) I	V (Horse) Gemini	Sagittarius (Rat) XI
Cancer(Sheep)VI	Scorpion (Pig) X	Fishes (Rabbit) II	VI (Sheep) Cancer	Capricorn(Buffalo)XII
			VII (Monkey) Lion	Aquarius (Tiger) I
			VIII(Rooster)Virgin	Fishes (Rabbit) II

Maximized familism		Minimized familism	
March (Dragon) Aries	Virgin (Rooster) August	March (Dragon) Aries	Fishes (Rabbit) February
April (Snake) Taurus	Lion (Monkey) July	April (Snake) Taurus	Aquarius (Tiger) January
May (Horse) Gemini	Cancer (Sheep) June	May (Horse) Gemini	Capricorn(Buffalo)December
September (Dog) Libra	Fishes (Rabbit) February	June (Sheep) Cancer	Sagittarius(Rat)November
October (Pig) Scorpion	Aquarius (Tiger) January	July (Monkey) Lion	Scorpion (Pig) October
November(Rat)Sagittarius	Capricorn(Buffalo)December	August(Rooster)Virgin	Libra (Dog) September

Each day is characterized with: - illuminating examples, in the religious calendar
- a phrase, in the Theban zodiac

For the compatibilities of this zodiac we use the Chinese day, the numerology of the day and the compatibilities of the degrees of the classical zodiac signs.

Maximized monachism			Minimized monachism	
decan 1 Aries	decan 1 Lion	decan 1 Sagittarius	decan 1 Aries	decan 1 Libra
decan 2 Aries	decan 2 Lion	decan 2 Sagittarius	decan 2 Aries	decan 2 Libra
decan 3 Aries	decan 3 Lion	decan 3 Sagittarius	decan 3 Aries	decan 3 Libra
decan 1 Taurus	decan 1 Virgin	decan 1 Capricorn	decan 1 Taurus	decan 1 Scorpion
decan 2 Taurus	decan 2 Virgin	decan 2 Capricorn	decan 2 Taurus	decan 2 Scorpion
decan 3 Taurus	decan 3 Virgin	decan 3 Capricorn	decan 3 Taurus	decan 3 Scorpion
decan 1 Gemini	decan 1 Libra	decan 1 Aquarius	decan 1 Gemini	decan 1 Sagittarius
decan 2 Gemini	decan 2 Libra	decan 2 Aquarius	decan 2 Gemini	decan 2 Sagittarius
decan 3 Gemini	decan 3 Libra	decan 3 Aquarius	decan 3 Gemini	decan 3 Sagittarius
decan 1 Cancer	decan 1 Scorpion	decan 1 Fishes	decan 1 Cancer	decan 1 Capricorn
decan 2 Cancer	decan 2 Scorpion	decan 2 Fishes	decan 2 Cancer	decan 2 Capricorn
decan 3 Cancer	decan 3 Scorpion	decan 3 Fishes	decan 3 Cancer	decan 3 Capricorn
degree 0 Cancer	degree 0 Scorpion	degree 0 Fishes	decan 1 Lion	decan 1 Aquarius
degree 1 Cancer	degree 1 Scorpion	degree 1 Fishes	decan 2 Lion	decan 2 Aquarius
degree 2 Cancer	degree 2 Scorpion	degree 2 Fishes	decan 3 Lion	decan 3 Aquarius
degree 3 Cancer	degree 3 Scorpion	degree 3 Fishes	decan 1 Virgin	decan 1 Fishes
degree 4 Cancer	degree 4 Scorpion	degree 4 Fishes	decan 2 Virgin	decan 2 Fishes
degree 5 Cancer	degree 5 Scorpion	degree 5 Fishes	decan 3 Virgin	decan 3 Fishes
degree 6 Cancer	degree 6 Scorpion	degree 6 Fishes	degree 0 Virgin	degree 0 Fishes
degree 7 Cancer	degree 7 Scorpion	degree 7 Fishes	degree 1 Virgin	degree 1 Fishes
degrees: 8-8-8; 9-9-9; 10-10-10; 11-11-11; 12-12-12; 13-13-13; 14-14-14; 15-15-15; 16-16-16; 17-17-17; 19-19-19; 20-20-20; 21-21-21; 22-22-22; 23-23-23; 24-24-24; 25-25-25; 26-26-26; 27-27-27; 28-28-28; 29-29-29			degrees: 2-2; 3-3; 4-4; 5-5; 6-6; 7-7; 8-8; 9-9; 10-10; 11-11; 12-12; 13-13; 14-14; 15-15; 16-16; 17-17; 18-18;19-19; 20-20; 21-21; 22-22;23-23;24-24;25-25;26-26;27-27;29-29	

Maximized familism		Minimized familism	
decan 1 (Dragon) Aries	decan 3 Virgin (Rooster)	decan 1 (Dragon) Aries	decan 3 Fishes (Rabbit)
decan 2 (Dragon) Aries	decan 2 Virgin (Rooster)	decan 2 (Dragon) Aries	decan 2 Fishes (Rabbit)
decan 3 (Dragon) Aries	decan 1 Virgin (Rooster)	decan 3 (Dragon) Aries	decan 1 Fishes (Rabbit)
decan 1 (Snake) Taurus	decan 3 Lion (Monkey)	decan 1 (Snake) Taurus	decan 3 Aquarius (Tiger)
decan 2 (Snake) Taurus	decan 2 Lion (Monkey)	decan 2 (Snake) Taurus	decan 2 Aquarius (Tiger)
decan 3 (Snake) Taurus	decan 1 Lion (Monkey)	decan 3 (Snake) Taurus	decan 1 Aquarius (Tiger)
decan 1 (Horse) Gemini	decan 3 Cancer (Sheep)	decan 1 (Horse) Gemini	decan 3 Capricorn (Buffalo)
decan 2 (Horse) Gemini	decan 2 Cancer (Sheep)	decan 2 (Horse) Gemini	decan 2 Capricorn (Buffalo)
decan 3 (Horse) Gemini	decan 1 Cancer (Sheep)	decan 3 (Horse) Gemini	decan 1 Capricorn (Buffalo)
decan 1 (Dog) Libra	decan 3 Fishes (Rabbit)	decan 1 (Sheep) Cancer	decan 3 Sagittarius (Rat)
decan 2 (Dog) Libra	decan 2 Fishes (Rabbit)	decan 2 (Sheep) Cancer	decan 2 Sagittarius (Rat)
decan 3 (Dog) Libra	decan 1 Fishes (Rabbit)	decan 3 (Sheep) Cancer	decan 1 Sagittarius (Rat)
decan 1 (Pig) Scorpion	decan 3 Aquarius (Tiger)	decan 1 (Monkey) Lion	decan 3 Scorpion (Pig)
decan 2 (Pig) Scorpion	decan 2 Aquarius (Tiger)	decan 2 (Monkey) Lion	decan 2 Scorpion (Pig)
decan 3 (Pig) Scorpion	decan 1 Aquarius (Tiger)	decan 3 (Monkey) Lion	decan 1 Scorpion (Pig)
decan 1 (Rat) Sagittarius	decan 3 Capricorn (Buffalo)	decan 1 (Rooster) Virgin	decan 3 Libra (Dog)
decan 2 (Rat) Sagittarius	decan 2 Capricorn (Buffalo)	decan 2 (Rooster) Virgin	decan 2 Libra (Dog)
decan 3 (Rat) Sagittarius	decan 1 Capricorn (Buffalo)	decan 3 (Rooster) Virgin	decan 1 Libra (Dog)
degree 0 (Rat)Sagittarius	degree 29 Capricorn(Buffalo)	degree 0 (Rooster) Virgin	degree 29 Libra (Dog)
degree 1 (Rat)Sagittarius	degree 28 Capricorn(Buffalo)	degree 1 (Rooster) Virgin	degree 28 Libra (Dog)
degrees: 2-27; 3-26; 4-25; 5-24; 6-23; 7-22; 8-21; 9-20; 10-19;11-18; 12-17; 13-16; 14-15		degrees: 2-27; 3-26; 4-25; 5-24; 6-23; 7-22; 8-21; 9-20; 10-19;11-18; 12-17; 13-16; 14-15	

The Vedic Indian Persian, Druidic Celtic Arboreal, African, Egyptian, floral American intercontinental and the Apache American Indian zodiacs comparatively with the **classical zodiac**, everyone's zodiacal compatibility is that of the classical zodiac:

The decades of the classical zodiac with other constellations than the 12 ones	Vedic Indian Persian zodiac	Druidic Celtic Arboreal zodiac
decan 1 Aries(III 21 – III 30) Cassiopeia(enthroned crowned woman, queen)	Hatchet (III 21- III 31)	Oak (III 21) Hazelnut (III 22 - III 30)
decan 2 Aries(III 31- IV 9) Cetus(cetaceous, sea monster, Whale, leviathan)	Hatchet (III 31) Horse (IV 1 - IV 9)	Hazelnut (III 31) Rowan (IV 1 - IV 9)
decan 3 Aries(IV 10 – IV 20) Perseus(man and Medusa)	Horse (IV 10) Cabman (IV 11 - IV 20)	Rowan (IV 10) Maple (IV 11 - IV 20)
decan 1 Taurus(IV 21 – V 1) Orion(man with a shield and a branch, giant)	Fire (IV 21 - IV 30) Goat (V 1)	Walnut (IV 21 - IV 30) Poplar (V 1)
decan 2 Taurus(V 2 – V 10) Eridanus(River)	Goat (V 2 - V 10)	Poplar (V 2 - V 10)
decan 3 Taurus(V 11 – V 20) Auriga(cabman shepherd carrying a goat or a she-wolf)	Elephant (V 11 - V 20)	Poplar (V 11 - V 14) Chestnut (V 15 - V 20)
decan 1 Gemini(V 21 – V 31) Lepus(the Rabbit)	Thread (V 21- V 31)	Chestnut (V 20 - V 24) Ash (V 25 - V 31)
decan 2 Gemini(VI 1 – VI 10) Canis Major (the Big Dog)	Phoenix (VI 1 - VI 10)	Ash (VI 1 - VI 3) Hornbeam (VI 4 - VI 10)
decan 3 Gemini(VI 11 – VI 21) Canis Minor(the Small Dog)	Diamonds(VI 11 - VI 20) Boar (VI 21)	Hornbeam (VI 11 -VI 13) Fig (VI 14 - VI 21)
decan 1 Cancer(VI 22 – VII 1) Ursa Minor (the Lesser, Small Bear, She-Bear, Dipper, Fold, Plough, Plow, Wain or Wagon)	Boar (VI 22 - VI 30) Snake (VII 1)	Fig (VI 22 - VI 23) Birch (VI 24) Apple (VI 25 - VII 1)
decan 2 Cancer(VII 2 – VII 12) Ursa Major(the Greater, Big Bear)	Snake (VII 2 - VII 10) Turtle (VII 11 - VII 12)	Apple (VII 2 - VII 4) Fir (VII 5 - VII 13)
decan 3 Cancer(VII 13 – VII 22) Argo(the Ark)	Turtle (VII 13 - VII 21) Dog (VII 22)	Fir (VII 14) Elm (VII 15 - VII 22)
decan 1 Lion(VII 23 - VIII 2) Hydra(the Hydra, aquatic monster or snake)	Dog (VII 23 - VIII 1) Migrator (VIII 2)	Elm (VII 23 - VII 25) Cypress (VII 26 - VIII 2)
decan 2 Lion(VIII 3 - VIII 12) Crater(the Crater, Cup)	Migrator (VIII 3-VIII 12)	Cypress (VIII 3 - VIII 4) Poplar (VIII 5 - VIII 12)
decan 3 Lion(VIII 13 - VIII 22) Corvus(the Crow, Raven)	Bear (VIII 13 - VIII 22)	Poplar (VIII 13) Cedar (VIII 14 - VIII 22)
decan 1 Virgin(VIII 23 - IX 2) Coma(the Mane, Hair)	Bear (VIII 23) Virgin (VIII 24 - IX 2)	Cedar (VIII 23) Pine (VIII 24 - IX 2)
decan 2 Virgin(IX 3 - IX 12) Centaurus(the Centaur)	Feather (IX 3 - IX 12)	Willow (IX 3 - IX 12)
decan 3 Virgin(IX 13 - IX 22) Bootes(the bear, the dog, shepherd, pastor, ploughman, plowman)	Swallow (IX 13 - IX 22)	Lime (IX 13 - IX 22)
decan 1 Libra(IX 23 - X 2) Crux Australis (the Austral or Southern Cross)	Swallow (IX 23) Balance (IX 24 - X 2)	Olive (IX 23) Hazelnut (IX 24 - X 2)
decan 2 Libra(X 3 - X 13) Lupus(the Wolf near the Centaur)	Balance (X 3) Hawk (X 4 - X 13)	Hazelnut (X 3) Rowan (X 4 - X 13)
decan 3 Libra(X 14 - X 23) Corona Borealis(the Boreal or Northern Crown)	Monkey (X 14 - X 23)	Maple (X 14 - X 23)

The decades of the classical zodiac with other constellations than the 12 ones	Vedic Indian Persian zodiac	Druidic Celtic Arboreal zodiac
decan 1 Scorpion(X 24 - XI 2) Serpens(the Snake grasped by Ophiuchus)	Dolphin (X 24 - XI 2)	Walnut (X 24 - XI 2)
decan 2 Scorpion(XI 3 - XI 12) Ophiuchus(Serpentarius, man grasping a serpent and with a foot on the Scorpion)	Tower (XI 3 - XI 12)	Plop (XI 3 - XI 11) Chestnut (XI 12)
decan 3 Scorpion(XI 13 - XI 21) Hercules(man on one knee, holding a branch and with the other foot over the head of the Dragon) with Cerberus(snake or dog with 3 heads)	Lion (XI 13 - XI 21)	Chestnut (XI 13 - XI 21)
decan 1 Sagittarius(XI 22- XII 1) Lyra(vulture holding a Lyre)	Lion (XI 22) Hermit (XI 23 - XII 1)	Ash (XI 22 - XII 1)
decan 2 Sagittarius(XII 2 - XII 11) Ara(the Altar)	Hermit (XII 2) Schell (XII 3 - XII 11)	Hornbeam(XII 2 -XII 11)
decan 3 Sagittarius(XII 12 - XII 21) Drago(Dragon, reptile or serpent)	Schell (XII 12) Metal (XII 13 - XII 21)	Fig (XII 12 - XII 21)
decan 1 Capricorn(XII 22 - XII 31) Sagitta Australis(an Austral, Southern arrow)	Cordage (XII 22-XII 31)	Beech (XII 22) Apple (XII 23 - XII 31)
decan 2 Capricorn(I 1 - I 10) Aquila(the Eagle with the Septentrional, Northern Arrow)	Lotus (I 1 - I 10)	Apple (I 1) Fir (I 2 - I 10)
decan 3 Capricorn(I 11 - I 19) Delphinus(the Dolphin bursting out of the water)	Archer (I 11 - I 19)	Fir (I 11) Elm (I 12 - I 19)
decan 1 Aquarius(I 20 - I 29) Pisces Australis(the Austral or Southern Fish)	Archer (I 20) Vulture (I 21 - I 29)	Elm (I 20 - I 24) Cypress (I 25 - I 29)
decan 2 Aquarius(I 30 - II 8) Pegasus(winged horse)	Vulture (I 30) Chariot (I 31 - II 8)	Cypress (I 30 - II 3) Poplar (II 4 - II 8)
decan 3 Aquarius(II 9 - II 18) Cygnus(the Swan)	Chariot (II 9) Water (II 10 - II 18)	Date (II 9 - II 18)
decan 1 Fishes(II 19 - II 29) Linum(two lines, bridles that link the two Fishes' zodiacal sign constellation with Cetus)	Water (II 19) Pearl (II 20 - II 29)	Pine (II 19 - II 27) Willow (II 28 - II 29)
decan 2 Fishes(III 1 - III 10) Cepheus(man with a scepter and a crown, king)	Pearl (III 1) Ship (III 2 - III 10)	Willow (III 1 - III 10)
decan 3 Fishes(III 11 - III 20) Andromeda(woman)	Meditator (III 11 - III 20)	Lime (III 11- III 20)

These zodiacs show the variation of the periods, by the shifts or intertwinements of the zodiac signs.

Classical zodiac	African zodiac	Vedic zodiac	Egyptian zodiac	Floral American intercontinental zodiac	Apache American Indian zodiac
aries (III 21-IV 20) ♈	Donyan gabetoyo(III) , Pewarkomba(Uwokumba)(IV) (the migration is ending, big grass)	Meena (III 21- IV 14), Mesha (lamb) (IV 15 – IV 20)	Nile (river) (III 21- III 26), Bastet (feline, cat) (III 27 – IV 20)	alpinia (III 21), flamboyant flower (III 21 – IV 20), lady's slipper orchid (III 20)	falcon (kestrel,tiercel, merlin, hobby) (III 21- IV 20)
taurus (IV 21 – V 20) ♉	Pewrkomba(Uwokumba)(IV-V) , Zenko (V) (the bushes are cut)	Mesha (IV 21 – V 15), Vrishbha (calf) (V 16 – V 20)	Bastet(IV 21 – IV 25), Anubis (canid, jackal, dog) (IV 26 – V 20)	flamboyant flower(IV 21), lady's slipper orchid (IV 21 – V 20), heliconia (V 20)	beaver (biber, breb, castor, nutria) (IV 21 – V 20)
gemini (V 21 – VI 21) ♊	Zenko(V-VI) , Zenwi(Zenwili) (VI) (the plantation's month)	Vrishbha (V 21 – VI 16), Mithum (twins) (VI 17 – VI 21)	Anubis(V 21 – V 25), Horus (harrier hawk) (V 26 – VI 21)	lady's slipper orchid (V 21), heliconia (V 21-VI 21), water hyacinth (VI 21)	stag(hind,hart, deer, doe, buck, elk, reindeer, caribou, forest cow, bull, ox, calf, fawn) (V 21 – VI 21)
cancer (VI 22– VII 22) ♋	Zenwi(Zenwili) (VI-VII), Fofo (VII) (storms, rains)	Mithum (VI 22 –VII 16), Karka (crab) (VII 17 –VII 22)	Horus(VI 22 – VI 24), Geb (the terrestrial Globe) (VI 25 – VII 22)	heliconia (VI 22) water hyacinth (VI 22 – VII 22) bird of paradise flower (VII 22)	woodpecker (hickwall, wickwall, yuccle) (VI 22– VII 22)
lion (VII 23-VIII 22) ♌	Fofo (VII-VIII), Mboro (VIII) (the groundnuts are drawn out and the sweet potatoes are planted)	Karka (VII 23 - VIII 17), Simha (lion) (VIII 18-VIII 22)	Geb(VII 22 – VII 25), Amon (Sun) (VII 26 – VIII 22)	water hyacinth (VII 23), bird of paradise flower (VII 23 – VIII 22), yellow shrimp flower (VIII 22)	salmon (hunchon, huchon, trout, pastruga, kaluga, nisetru, beluga, sturgeon) (VII 23-VIII 22)
virgin (VIII 23-IX 22) ♍	Mboro(VIII-IX), Lisi (Yesi) (IX) (the crops' weeding, rites)	Simha (VIII 23- 17 IX) Kanya (candid) (IX 18 – IX 22)	Amon(VIII23–VIII28), Isis (Moon) (VIII 29 – IX 22)	bird of paradise flower (VIII 23), yellow shrimp flower (VIII 23 – IX 22), red ginger lily (IX 22)	bear (she-bear, honey eater, denner, teddy, hibernator,cub) (VIII 23- IX 22)
libra (IX 23 – X 23) ♎	Lisi (Yesi (IX-X), Dagni(Kutukpu) (X) (the leaves are changing)	Kanya (IX 23 – X 17), Tula (balance) (X 18 – X 23)	Isis (IX 23 – IX 28), Nout (sky) (IX 29 – X 23)	yellow shrimp flower (IX 23), red ginger lily (IX 23–X 23), aloe(X 23)	raven (corbie, corby, crow, pie, magpie, jackdaw, daw, petrel, seagull, gull,gabian,albatross) (IX 23 - X 23)
scorpion (X 24 – XI 21) ♏	Dagni(Kutukpu)(X-XI), Babena (XI) (the first millet gives into ear, the grains are prepared, migration zones are shared, rites)	Tula (X 24 – XI 16), Vrishchika (sco.) (XI 17 – XI 21)	Nout (X 24 – X 27), Seth (desert) (X 28 – XI 21)	red ginger lily (X 24), aloe (X 24 – XI 21), hibiscus (XI 21)	snake (serpent, monster worm omida larva, undulating, skin shedder) (X 24 – XI 21)
sagittarius (XI 22– XII 21) ♐	Babena (XI-XII) , Wakawaka (XII) (the crop preparing and the New Year)	Vrishchika (XI 22 –XII 16), Dhanu (bow) (XII 17 –XII 21)	Seth(XI 22 – XI 26), Osiris (vegetation) (XI 27 – XII 21)	aloe (XI 22), hibiscus (XI 22 – XII 21), flamingo lily (21 XII)	owl (owlet, howler, hissing moggy, hooter, screech) (XI 22 –XII 21)
capricorn (XII 22 – I 20) ♑	Wakawaka (XII-I), Benze (I) (harvesting the millet, the migration begins)	Dhanu (XII 22 – I 14), Makara(capr. or) (I 15 – I 20)	Osiris(XII 22 –XII 26), Sekhnet (lioness) (27 XII- 20 I)	hibiscus (XII 22), flamingo lily (XII 22 – I 20), plumeria (I 20)	goose(gander, big duck, drake, small swan) (XII 22 – I 20)
aquarius (I 21 – II 18) ♒	Benze (I-II), Dogia (II) (the month of the torrid heat)	Makara(mermaid-triton-dolphin-shark-crocodile) (I 21 – II 13), Kumbha (aquar.) (II 14 – II 18)	Sekhnet(I 21 – I 25), Thot (ibis bird) (I 26 – II 18)	flamingo lily (I 21), plumeria (I 21 – II 18), alpinia (II 18)	otter (kalan, otor,otraz,vidra, luntra, floater, seal, morse,walrus,whale, cachalot, cetacean) (I 21 – II 18)
fishes (II 19 – III 20) ♓	Dogia (II-III), Donyan gabetoyo (the honey is taken, the rain comes, the termites fly)	Kumbha (II 19 – III 14), Meena (fishes) (III 15 – III 20)	Thot (II 19 – II 24), Nile (II 25 – III 20)	plumeria (II 19), alpinia (II 19 – III 20), flamboyant flower (III 20)	wolf (she-wolf, lup, lupess, wolfling) (II 19 – III 20)

The center of the classical zodiac is the Earth; from here we observe the sky.

A zodiac cycle has 12 signs, extended on the 360 degrees of the zodiac circle.

A sign has 30 degrees,these are divided into 3 decans:the first decan has the 0-9 degrees, the second 10-19, the third 20-29, each of 10 degrees.
(deanship=decan=dean=deacon=deaconess=diocese=decennium=decade=decathlon=decalogue=10).

1 degree=60 minutes (horoscope=hora=hour in objectiv, zodiac=zoo circus)

1 minute=60 seconds

Our star, the Sun, our satellite, the Moon, the planets, their satellites, the planetoids, the asteroids and any other sky body, pass thru the 360 zodiac degrees (these form a circle=the zodiac circle=the ecliptic, that cuts the Earth oblique in report with the equator, it is the plan in which the Earth rotates itself around the Sun, the name ecliptic comes from the fact that in this plan the eclipses are frequent). According to the number of the degree thru which the sky object passes, we have that classical zodiacal sign. In the past the signs were the constellations (these had the form of the signs and still do), but in thousands of years from the realization of the classical zodiac, the solar system moved from those stars, so the signs now don't correspond with those stars, but with the parts of the universe.

The 12 classical zodiacal signs mean a powerful human body:

Aries	the head of a ram
Taurus	the neck of a bull
Gemini	the shoulders, the superior members to work at unison, as identical are the twins
Cancer	the sternum with the ribs, the thorax, like the hard armor of the crawfish, crayfish, lobster
Lion	the heart and the spinal cord of a lion
Virgin	the abdomen to be supple like at a virgin
Libra	the kidneys and the hips to move themselves as smooth as a balance
Scorpion	the secretor organs, the bladder, the urethra that have the shape and force of a scorpion
Sagittarius	strong thighs like those of the taurus with a human body, the centaur
Capricorn	the knees, the articulations, the bones, to be hard like at a wild goat
Aquarius	healthy shanks, that mustn't accumulate liquid, like two pots from which the water flows
Fishes	agile soles like two fish

A classical zodiac has two components:

- one in which we consider the zodiac's center of observation, the center of Earth (this being the center of the zodiac circle), neglecting the movement of rotation around its own axis. Our classical zodiacal signs (solar, the most known from all the publications, of the Moon, of each planet, of the planetoids, asteroids or even more) taken from the zodiac circle that traverses the Earth, are described at the transposition of the Chinese zodiac over the classical one.

- another one in which we take into account the fact that we are not in the center of Earth, but on its surface. The terrestrial Globe rotates around its own axis, so practically every day we pass thru the degrees of the zodiacal circle. We are interested in what signs were the sky bodies, at the moment and place of birth of a person. Consequently a new circle appears, named the houses circle(12 houses, with the significance of the 12 signs, equal between them), this circle is perpendicular on the place of birth, so crosses the Earth, on the direction east-west and zenith-nadir(zenith=the perpendicular on the place of birth, the point on the sky above the head of a standing up person, nadir=the prolonging of this perpendicular, thru Earth on the opposite side of it, the point on the opposite sky to the place of birth). Now we project this circle of the 12 houses (a house will occupy one or more signs from the zodiacal circle) on the zodiacal circle(which is approximately in the Equator's plan, described at the transposal of the Chinese zodiac over the classical one) and we see that these houses, become unequal on the zodiacal circle, also the east-west axis is perpendicular on the zenith-nadir axis on the circle of the houses, and in the circle of the zodiac the two axes will form other angles between it(as the shadows of the windows=the houses' circle, are projected on the floor=the zodiac circle). These two overlapping circles are the result of a look on the axis that is perpendicular on the zodiac's circle, forming the map of the horoscope. By this way we find in which signs are each of the 12 houses(a house will occupy one or more signs of the zodiacal circle), so also in what signs are the 4 directions from the wanted place and moment.

The description of the houses and the 4 main directions that these contain:

- the ascendant=the rise=the East (the celestial point from where the Sun is rising, tracked down thru calculations or by the direct observation of the sky at the place and moment of birth; the energies of the sky's vault invade the new born, there are also a little diminished energies, that come from the opposite part of the place of birth, so those that go thru Earth to arrive at the baby, but from the east come the majority of the energies from the universe, because those are sucked by the movement from west to east of the terrestrial Globe around its own axis)

- the descendant=the set=the West at the place and time of birth (the opposite point of the ascendant)

- the middle of the sky=midheaven=zenith=the South (we find it down, at south on the map of the horoscope, on the projection of the houses' circle on the circle of the zodiac that gives the horoscope; some say it is the maximum point of the ascension of the Sun on the sky, so the middle of the day, the noon, different from the definition of the zenith, the perpendicular on the place of birth, but projected on the circle of the zodiac both would be into the same plan)

- the bottom of the sky=imum coeli=nadir=the North (the opposite point to the middle of the sky)

The 12 astrological houses are named like this because we also have in the real life a house, the inhabitants of those 12 houses are the celestial bodies. These houses are separated by lines, named cuspids(the fences between the houses; a cake cut in 12 pieces or a valve with 12 cusps viewed from above),some of these cuspids being the 4 directions: the ascendant, descendent, middle and bottom of the sky:

the named cusps and the houses		symbolize the
E=*ascendant* = the cusp of house I = the line between the houses XII and I,	House I	Aries
	House II	Taurus
	House III	Gemini
N=*bottom of the sky*=cusp of house IV=the line between the houses III and IV,	House IV	Cancer
	House V	Lion
	House VI	Virgin
W=*descendant*=the cusp of house VII=the line between the houses VI and VII,	House VII	Libra
	House VIII	Scorpio
	House IX	Sagittarius
S=*middle of the sky*=cusp of house X=the line between the houses IX and X,	House X	Capricorn
	House XI	Aquarius
	House XII	Fishes

Knowing the 4 directions at that place and moment, we thus know the ascendant(the east), so the other 3 named cusps and all the 12 houses too. By projecting this circle of the houses over the zodiac's circle, we see in what signs are the 4 cuspides and the houses. There are lots of complicated methods of calculation, I described further on their principles.

In the ephemeredes tables (these are named like that because the tables are ephemeral: the Earth, the solar system, our galaxy being in continuous movement). We can create them because the astronomers can mathematically predict the trajectories of the objects of the sky, the astrologers project their motion: on the zodiacal circle and into the ephemeredes tables. In these tables we find the calendar years and the movements of the sky bodies at a moment of a day(in general at the universal hour=GMT 00, but there also tables for the hour 12): of the Sun, of the Moon, of the planets, of planetoid Chiron, of the Moon's north and south nods and of the black Moon(Lilith), all being described at the transposal of the Chinese zodiac over the classical one; these have a certain regularity, but in thousands and millions of years all their movements will differ, that is why it is needed all the time the astronomical observation.

Thru the ephemeredes tables we can see our: solar zodiacal sign, vulcanian, mercurian, venusian, lunar, of the Moon's nods, of the black Moon, martian, jupiterian, saturnian, neptunian, of planetoid Chiron, uranian, plutonian, of the different planetoids, asteroids or of other planets' satellites from the solar system. We also find in these tables the sidereal=stellar=astral time. Free internet addresses with the ephemeredes tables:

www.astro.com/swisseph/swepha_e.htm

www.findyourfate.com/astrology/ephemeris

Thus when we are born we are not just a zodiacal sign, the solar one(Aries, for example), but at the same time we are other signs too(for example: martian Cancer-when Mars passes thru the degrees of the zodiacal circle that correspond to the cancer sign, neptunian Gemini-when Neptune passes thru the degrees of the Gemini, and so on for each planet, Moon nod, satellites, asteroids).

The movement in the solar system can be found:

- directly thru the help of computers connected to the astronomical observatories, the artificial satellites, the space derricks or to the space shuttles

- thru mathematical calculi based on the astronomical data, these are concentrated in the ephemeredes tables (the virtual point of observation in these, being the center of the Earth)

- thru computer programs based on calculi or upon the ephemeredes tables

The ascendant is calculated after the principles:

- with the standard hour and date = standard time = winter time, the results depend on the longitude and latitude of the birth place, then the standard time is transformed in:

G   Genesis Genome Galaxy Grace from God Globe Gentle Greenwich

M Monastic Marriage Matrimonial Marital Materialization Mapping Measurer Meridian

T   Tender Telluric Transpacific Therapeutic Time

universal solar hour and date = the hour of London's or Greenwich's meridian, not London's or Greenwich's hour, cause there too is the summer time; to which we add the:

- sidereal GMT hour=stellar=astral, from the ephemeredes tables

From another table, that shows the repartition of the zodiacal signs over the sidereal clock's hours, it is found the ascendant.

The calculus of the ascendant can be made with the official hour and date at the immediately specified internet addresses (so with the daylight saving time=summer time=summer hour and date).

The official hour and date = official time = legal time = legal hour and date = the calendar hour and date = the hour from the register from the hospital of birth and the date from the identity documents, so it represents both the daylight saving hour and date and the standard hour and date.

The GMT hour and date = universal earthly solar time of birth = the Universal Coordinated Time, this measures in how much time a point from Earth sees again the Sun (24 hours). If we are not born at the GMT meridian(this passes from the north pole to the south pole thru Greenwich, a locality near London, dividing approximately in two the GMT zone), we take a map of the time zones and we see in what time zone we were born and we subtract the eventual daylight saving time, and then we subtract the number of hours that separates us from the GMT hour(if we are on the left side,-, of the GMT) or we add the hours(if we are on the right,+, of the GMT); the GMT date and hour, can change with one day in plus or in minus, even with a month(if we are in the first or the last day of it) or even a year (if we are on January 1 or December 31).

The sidereal hour and date (in Latin sideris=star) = stellar = astral GMT, with reference points the Sun and a relatively fixed star. The sidereal time measures in how much time the Earth rotates completely(360 degrees) around it's own axis(in how much time a point on Earth sees again the same star) and it is in the ephemeredes tables but only for the hour 00, using the three simple rule we find the results for our standard hour(not of summer) and with another table we find out the ascendant. On Earth we measure the GMT time and the local time with a delay of less than 4 minutes (3 minutes and 56 seconds), because we don't measure in how much time the Earth rotates around it's own axis, but in how much time the light of the Sun sees again a same point on Earth(24 hours). These approximately 4 minutes in plus of the GMT, from the sidereal time, are due to the fact that the Earth makes a rotation around the Sun at the same time with the rotation on its own axis.

Also the ascendants have decades, degrees, minutes(being a zodiacal sign).

When the ascendant of a person is compatible with the another's, the houses and the rest of the cusps will be mathematically compatible in a bigger proportion.

Because of the many tables, I didn't give the methods of calculations, but neither the simpler ones, because there are made all the time mistakes. At the next free internet addresses can be found the zodiacal signs, the ascendant and the other cuspids, very exactly (here we don't have to change by ourselves the date and hour according to the eventual daylight saving time, because this thing can be made automatically, so we introduce the date of birth from the identity card and the official hour from the register of the hospital of the birth, unlike at the calculation of the Chinese pillars where we have to transform): www.astro.com

www.astro-software.com

www.0800-horoscope.com/birthchart.php

We can compare the compatibility of a person with another or of an event with another for each of the signs(solar, vulcanian, mercurian…) and also for the ascendants. Thus we take the Sun's zodiacal sign for the first person and we compare it with the Sun's zodiacal sign of the other person, the Vulcan's zodiacal sign of the first person with that of the second person and so on for the other planets, satellites, asteroids and also the ascendants of the two persons.

How we can practically make the zodiacal compatibilities, by using the described theoretical data, it is exemplified at the total final zodiacal compatibility.

The Numerology and the Numbers

Maximized monachism (and a floral zodiac that corresponds to the numbers)			Minimized monachism		Maximized familism		Minimized familism	
1(10;19;28;sunflower)	5(14;23;iris)	9(18;27;rose)	1; 5; 9	3; 7	1;3;7;9	2; 8	1; 7	4
2(11;20;29;peony)	6(15;24;poppy)		2; 6	4; 8	3; 5; 9	4	2; 8	5
3(12;21;30;lady's slipper)	7(16;25;orchid)				1; 5; 7	6	3; 9	6
4(13;22;31;cornflower)	8(17;26;marguerite)							

- calendar day 10⇔1+0=1, day 19⇔1+9=10⇔1+0=1, day 14⇔1+4=5

In the numerology books there are all the details of the day, month, year of birth, destiny number, name numbers (for the names there are different tables where a letter has a number) and the grilles or grids with all the numbers. In essence we add cipher by cipher until we obtain a single number from 1 to 9. For the zodiacal compatibility of two people we find all of these numbers for each and then we compare them.

Some calculi in numerology:
The number of the day(we add the ciphers=figures=digits of the day until we obtain one figure, 29⇔2+9=11⇔1+1=2, the signification is of all the numbers), the same for the number of the month and the number of the year. We use for the zodiacal compatibilities also the Chinese pillars and the other zodiacs. There are also the numbers of the other divisions of the time.
The number of the whole date of birth=life (path) number=our destiny number = lesson number (we add the numbers until we obtain a single cipher: IV-2-1920 ⇔4+2+1+9+2+0=18 ⇔ 1+8=9).
The personal numbers are given by adding the date of birth to the current or desired date.

A numerological grille, looks like this (it is like the fengshui grille, but there the calculi and significances differ):

1	4	7
2	5	8
3	6	9

-for April(4) the 2nd 1920=>
4+2+1+9+2+0=18 is the intermediary number =>1+8=9=the life number
Some put into the grille the plain date of birth(4-2-1920):

1	4	
2;2		
		9

Others ad into the grid the number of life(here 9):

1	4	
2;2		
		9;9

Some also the intermediary number(here 18):

1;1	4	
2;2		8
		9;9

Others add other numbers, for example: April(4)-2-1920=> 4+2+1+9+2+0=18=the first intermediary number=>1+8=9=the number of life(sometimes we obtain directly this number, when this first intermediary number doesn't exist)18-2=16= the second intermediary number(obtained by subtracting from the first intermediary number or directly from the life number when the first intermediary number does not exist, the figure of the calendar day, if the days are:1,2,3..9, here the day is 2, so we subtract 2 from the first intermediate number, if the day would have been 5, we would have subtracted 5 from the first intermediate number; for the days 10, 11,...19 we subtract the first figure of those multiplied by two, cause these days have 2 figures, 1x2=2, so we subtract here 2 from the first intermediary number; for the days 20,21,...29, 2x2, we subtract thus 4 from the first intermediate number; for the days 30 and 31 3x2=6, we subtract 6 from the first intermediate number; if the result is with minus we consider it plus), the last number 1+6=7=the duty number(after some, if this number is bigger than 9, so 10,11,12,13…, we don't reduce it to a digit; also sometimes we obtain directly this number, respectively when this is a figure, without the second intermediary number):

1;1;1	4	7
2;2		8
	6	9;9

These are just a few types of calculations(there are also different figures of planets, that can be added). In general, the official date of birth is used, but also the transformed ones can be used.

The name has lots of numbers and possibilities of numbering the letters, in function of the form or the order of the letters in the alphabet.
We add the ciphers of the letters according to the type of number.
Some of the name numbers are the:
-cipher of the consonants=exterior=personality
-cipher of the vocals=interior=heart
-cipher of the family names=ancestors=genealogy
-cipher of the given names=intimate
-cipher of the entire name=some call it destiny number
There can also be used the lost or gained names.
We put the numbers of the name in a grille of 9 figures too.

We can over pose the grille of the birth date over that of the name.

It can be compared the grille of one person with the same type of grille of the other person, square with square, how many numbers are in one's square, how many numbers in the same square of the grille of the other one. For the zodiacal compatibility of two persons, we compare a type of number with the same type of number of the other person. Some of the numbers can be found for free also at the following internet address: http://astrology.newkerala.com/numerology

Number	Floral Zodiac	Shamanism	Cards	Tarot	Cabalah	Runes	Alchemy	Aura
0 (origin)	flower	animal	card,creature,joker,clown,buffoon	letter	letter	hieroglyph	element	colour
1	sunflower	monkey	ace,mirror, reflection, human being	magician	Aleph (A, bull)	Ansuz(ass, jack,jackass,jenny burro,colt,fillies, foals,donkeys, maryiskaya)	gold	all colors
2	peony	owl dolphin	11, 1 + 1 = 2 knight,knave, duchess,duke, juvenile,jack	high priestess	Beth (B, barrack, building)	Hagalaz (hails glacial)	water	bordeau black white
3	lady's slipper	dove	12, 1 + 2 = 3 prelates, parents, child, page,leaders, prince, princess, duchess, duke,lama, vodeasă, vodă,lamo, voievodeasă, pope, voievod,,popess crăiasă, crai, papess, mister, madam,papa, miss,sir,lady, lad, queen, king	empress	Gimel (G, camel)	Uruz (bulls, buffaloes, taurus)	earth water fire air	pink blue golden black red white
4	cornflower	eagle whale ram	13, 1 + 3 = 4 queen,king regal,royal	emperor	Daleth (D, door)	Dagaz (days)	fire	red orange
5	iris	bull elephant	5	high priest	Heh (H, hole window)	Raidho (ride, hippodrome)	earth	brown gray
6	poppy	duck snake lion	+/-VI stick:veli, clown	lovers	Vav (V, claw hook)	Wunjo (wish, joy)	vapors	rainbow red blue
7	orchid	crab horse falcon tortoise	VII	chariot	Zain(Z,link metal shirt)	Ehwaz (horses)	bronze silver gold	rainbow
8	marguerite	lion butterfly	VIII	justice, strength,force	Cheth(Ch, to encircle)	Elhaz (yew trees)	fire water	purply mauve
9	rose	squirrel snake reptiles	IX	hermit	Teth (T,serpent's tangue)	Jera (year, era)	earth gold	maroon yellow green

Special numbers in numerology that are reduced rarely to a single cipher, these numbers are containing the same cipher, the significance is of that cipher multiplied with the number of repetitions and of the result(222=2x3=6):

11,111,1111,11111,111111,1111111,11111111,111111111,1111111111,11111111111,111111111111,1111111111111....
22,222,2222,22222,222222,2222222,22222222,222222222,2222222222,22222222222,222222222222,2222222222222....
33,333,3333,33333,333333,3333333,33333333,333333333,3333333333,33333333333,333333333333,3333333333333....
44,444,4444,44444,444444,4444444,44444444,444444444,4444444444,44444444444,444444444444,4444444444444....
55,555,5555,55555,555555,5555555,55555555,555555555,5555555555,55555555555,555555555555,5555555555555....
66,666,6666,66666,666666,6666666,66666666,666666666,6666666666,66666666666,666666666666,6666666666666....
77,777,7777,77777,777777,7777777,77777777,777777777,7777777777,77777777777,777777777777,7777777777777....
88,888,8888,88888,888888,8888888,88888888,888888888,8888888888,88888888888,888888888888,8888888888888....
99,999,9999,99999,999999,9999999,99999999,999999999,9999999999,99999999999,999999999999,9999999999999....

Some of these are exemplified here:

11(1+1=2)	sunflower; peony	humming bird	juvenile,jack, queen,king, knight,knave, duchess, duke	truth, veridical, judgment	Kaph (K, hand kick, palm)	Tiwaz (terrestrial vastness)	air diamonds	azure blue white
22(2+2=4)	peony; cornflower	owl	creature	buffoon, clown, harlequin, jester, kinetism, movement	Tau (truncate, trim, cut)	Fehu (cattle)	air	white light
33(3+3=6) (33 vertebrae, weeks)	lady's slipper; poppy	pelican	marriage, vitalism, life, birth	star of the magical marital immaculate conception	Gimel; Vav	Laguz (lakes)	air, water emerald	opalescent white light

The playing cards:			
4 (seasons, on the ace) x 13(moon phases or rotative cyclical menstruations/year = type of cards) = 52 (weeks/year = cards) x 7days = 354 + 1 Joker (days/year)			
seasons and cardinal points	spring East	summer South	autumn West	winter North
the clans of the Amerindians	frog	sharpie hawk	turtle	butterfly
the elements of the classical signs	water ♋♏♓	fire ♈♌♐	earth ♉♍♑	air ♊♎♒
China, India, Persia, Italy, Spain, Portugal	cup	ring, money, gold	sword	baton, stick, truncheon
Central Europe (32 or 36 cards)	hearts	round bells	picked leaves	acorn
Europe and World (52 cards + 1, 2 or 3 Jokers)	pit, hole, grotto, crater with lava, red hearts, cup, grail, goblet with the nectar of the red grapes, receptacle, chalices	diamonds, rhomb, star, pentacles, pentagon, pollen, petals, seeds in capsule	spades, thorns, spikes, swords bit, black hearts, green yellow brown black leaves	shamrock, trefoil, triangle, trunk, cross, clubs, clover, maces, scepters, staff, branch, batons, bar, wands, pistils, stamina
	ţurcă, cricket, oină, baseball, tennis, hockey, skating, ski, cross, polo, golf, pool, bowling, petanque, volley, handball, basket, rugby, football, effort			

The numbers and their short signification:	Some of the interpretations of the numbers thru the classical zodiac			
0 egg nothing exists without God, everything	The most accepted variant	In increasing order the distance of the Moon, the planets, Pluto and the Sun from Earth, when all are in a straight line.	Variant	Variant
1 independence, unification	lion Sun	Moon Pluto is at the maximum distance from Earth, but being the 10th (in this row), it has also the cipher 1, 10 ⇔ 1 + 0(infinity) = 1.	lion Sun	aries Mars, Mercury
2 in dependence, affection, association, education	cancer Moon	Venus	cancer Moon	taurus Vulcan, Moon
3 interdependence, expression, creativity, training, integrality	gemini and virgin Mercury	Mars	sagittarius Jupiter	gemeni Jupiter, Venus
4 stability, force, power, repartition, equilibrium, immortal, collegial, compatible	taurus and libra Venus	Mercury	aquarius Uranus	cancer, aries Earth
5 kinetics, kinematics, medicine, doctor, dear, darling, desire, freedom, liberty, loyalty, loyalism, pair, love, enamoured, enamored, marriage, marital, in love, in zodiacs	aries and scorpio Mars	Sun	gemini, virgin Mercur	lion, taurus Mercury, Venus
6 charm, pharmacy, tenderness, safety, remedy	fishes Neptune	Jupiter	taurus, libra Venus	virgin Venus
7 sapience, salvation, savior, sport, research, wisdom, perfectionism, pray, creed, character	aquarius Uranus	Saturn	fishes Neptune	libra, cancer Jupiter, Moon
8 optimization, efficaciousness, immortality, collegiality, the compatibilities	capricorn Saturn	Uranus	aquarius(Uranus) capricorn(Saturn) scorpio(Pluto)	scorpio, lion Saturn, Sun
9 newborn, new, birth, innovation, renovation, intelligence, altruism	sagittarius Jupiter	Neptune	aries(Mars)	virgin, sagittarius Sun,Moon,Jupiter
11(1+1=2) vision	lion; cancer	Moon, Pluto; Venus	lion, Sun; cancer, Moon	aquarius Uranus
22(2+2=4) formation	cancer; taurus, libra	Venus; Mercury	cancer, Moon; aquarius, Uranus;	aries, capricorn Mars, Saturn
33(3+3=6) harmony	gemini, virgin; fishes	Mars; Jupiter	sagittarius,Jupiter; taurus,libra,Venus	sagittarius, taurus Jupiter, Venus

The reversed order of the classical zodiac signs is seen also at the eras (1classical zodiac era=2160 years) of the classical astrology: thus approximately between 4000-2000 was the era of the taurus, 2000-0 the era of the aries, 0-2000 the era of the fishes, and between 2000-4000, so today, is the era of the aquarius, thus being possible to see the zodiacal compatibilities between the eras also.

The Zodiac of the Calendar Months

Calendar	Signification	Romanian folklore	Other calendars
I January(XI)	Ianus,Iana,Iatros,Genuar(entrance in labor,birth in squat genuflexion, genoflection, on four paws and laterally)	gerar(glacial glacier glazed frost frigorific)	Istri.,C.,Bosni.Her.,S.,Montenegrins,Macedonians,P.,U.,B.,R.: sijecanj (the serenade of sectioning splitting cutting smashing wood for fire)
II February(XII)	Februus(fever,festival),Flavian,Faun,Fauna,Fabia,Via, Lupus,Lupa,Lupan,Fărcaşi,Romulus,Remus,Dragobete	făurar,forjerar(forger,grill)	Bretons,Bretans,Britans,Britons,Gauls,Galaţi,Geţi:solmonath(soil, Sun) Magyar Hungarian: bojtelo(time for bearing the fasting lenten famine)
III March(I)	Marte, Mars, Ares(agriculture), Alator, Albiorics, Barecs,Balearicus,Condatis,Visucius,Segomo,Toutatis, Thineus,Marmar,Mater,Meourz,Meours,Martin,Maris, Mamer,Dochia,Dragomir,morse,bear,marine,marathon	mărţişor(alpine avens of the mountain, liman, tundra, pustă, pampas, plateau, plain, veldt, valley, vad, savannah, mangrove, marriage, placenta)	Bulgarian: martenitsa(marteniţa,martiniţa,mărţişor,monstruos tenia worm) Arabic: rabi al awwal(solar beneficient pluvial spring) Hebrew,Turkish: nisan(blooming,blossoming,budding,growing,lăstărire)
IV April(II)	Aphrodite(aprire,open,flowers appear,impregnation) Anchises(closed inflorescence) Aeneas(the coming of the heat of the Sun) Venus(veneration,verde,virginity,green,grain,gravidity)	prier(pray,prairie,steppe,taiga,rugă,propitious), florariu(first flowers)	French: I poissons en estuaires(fishes in estuaries) Bretons,Bretans,Britans,Britons,Galaţi: eostremonath(pasture,izlaz,imaş) Ukrainian,Russian,Slavic,Polish:kviten(flowering)
V May(III)	Maia the mother,Mercury the son Meilichios the father (Celvoinic)Castor, Poludeucheis(Prăslea) (Cosânzeana)Clutaemnestra, Helena(Ileana) (miracle,Dioscouri,Quadrigemini,Tindaride,pollination)	florar(flowers),frunzar(foliage)	Uralic,Sami,Lappic:toukokuu(sowing) Americans,Incas: aymuray(harvest)
VI June(IV)	Juno the mother, Jupiter the father Juventas the daughter (juvenile, junior, joviality, youth)	cireşar(cherries)	French: messidor(meadows golden plateaus) Istri.,C.,Bosni. Her.,S.,Montenegrins,Macedonians: lipanj(linden) Chinese,Japanese: VI, lotus and minatsuki(monsoon, water)
VII July(V)	Julius,Cesar,Cesara,Cezar,Julia,Caius,Gaius,Cleopatra, Cesaris, Caesarion, Cogaion, Cogaiona, Kogaionon, Cogiaionon,Kogaion,Kogheonon,Cogheonon,Cogheon, Cogiaion,Cogeonon,Cogeon,cognoscible	cuptor(cooker,oven,hatcher,brooder,incubator)	Chinese,Indochinese,Koreans,Mongols,Taiwanese,Japanese: VII Aleuts,Inuits,Eskimos: manniit(eggs) Icelanders,Danishes,Norwegians,Finns,Swedes:Solmanuour(Sun) French: thermidor(terrestrial solar heat heliotherapy temperature)
VIII August(VI)	Augustus, Octavius, Octavia, Augusta, Turin, Thurinus, Cezar,Cezara,Caius,Caia,Gaia,Gaius,Cegeton,Zigotum, Kogeonon,Coguaionan,Cogeuon,cognation	gustar(gustation,gustatory,taste)	French: fructidor(the citrons quinces gutuile golden auriferous apples pears apricots peaches prunes plums vegetables tomatoes solanaceae zarzavaturi) Zoroastrians: amordad(immortality)
IX September(VII)	Septimius,Septimia,Geta,sepals,the septation of the leaves from the branches, sepia halifron	răpciune(ragged leaves)	Arabic: ramadan(the gift of solar heat) Istri.,C.,Bosni. Her.,S.,Montenegrins,Macedonians: rujan(red)
X October(VIII)	Oceanus,Oceania,Oto,Octav,Octavia,octopoda	brumărel(small brume)	French: vendémiaire,vendange(holy vintage)
XI November(IX)	Noie,Noe,Nveioachim,Nveiacht,Naviac,Noemi, Naomi, new born from the human embryo, nautilus	brumar(brume)	Czechs,Slov.,Poles,L.,Estonians: listopad(leaves fall) French: brumaire(brume)
XII December(X)	Deceneu,Decebal,Deceangli,Deceanglia,decabracia	andrea,îndrea,undrea(needles for crocheting)	Bretons,Bretans,Britans,Britons,Gauls,Galaţi,Geţi: aerra geola(before frost)

Maximized monachism			Minimized monachism		Maximized familism		Minimized familism	
I	V	IX	I	VII	(III,3,tiger) I	X (pig,12,XII)	(III,3,tiger) I	IV (snake,6,VI)
II	VI	X	II	VIII	(IV,4,rabbit) II	IX (dog,11,XI)	(IV,4,rabbit) II	III (dragon,5,V)
III	VII	XI	III	IX	(V,5,dragon) III	VIII (rooster,10,X)	(VII,7,horse) V	XII (buffalo,2,II)
IV	VIII	XII	IV	X	(VI,6,snake) IV	VII (monkey,9,IX)	(VIII,8,sheep) VI	XI (rat,1,I)
			V	XI	(VII,7,horse) V	VI (sheep,8,VIII)	(IX,9,monkey) VII	X (pig,12,XII)
			VI	XII	(I,1,rat) XI	XII (buffalo,2,II)	(X,10,rooster) VIII	IX (dog,11,XI)

Discussions:

A research on ten million marriages, shows in the big majority approximately the same number, 70000 marriages x 12 x 12 months; the same for the classical solar signs. Thus it is showed that there isn't a significant increase of the marriages on the basis of the zodiacal compatibilities between the calendar months or the classical solar zodiac signs: www.ccsr.ac.uk/research/voasastrology.pdf

http://en.wikipedia.org/wiki/List_of_topics_characterized_as_pseudoscience

The Zodiac of the Calendar Years

It is given by a Baluchistanese Chinese Indian Iranian Tibetan zodiac with 12 zodiac signs. The year of this zodiac and the Asiatic Chinese year in Japan start at I 1.

Chinese Zodiac	Baltistanese Zodiac	The elements of the calendar years Tree earth, Fire metal, Earth water, Metal tree, Water fire
rat	yak herbs,green trulku of the buffalo	1900;1912;1924;1936;1948;1960;1972;1984;1996;2008;2020;2032;2044;2056;2068;2080;2092;2104;2116;2128;2140
buffalo	lunar,yellow trulku of the rat	1901;1913;1925;1937;1949;1961;1973;1985;1997;2009;2021;2033;2045;2057;2069;2081;2093;2105;2117;2129;2141
tiger	solar,red trulku of the pig	1902;1914;1926;1938;1950;1962;1974;1986;1998;2010;2022;2034;2046;2058;2070;2082;2094;2106;2118;2130;2142
rabbit	mammoth vegetables,black trulku of the dog	1903;1915;1927;1939;1951;1963;1975;1987;1999;2011;2023;2035;2047;2059;2071;2083;2095;2107;2119;2131;2143
dragon	dragonfly,kite,star,green trulku of the rooster	1904;1916;1928;1940;1952;1964;1976;1988;2000;2012;2024;2036;2048;2060;2072;2084;2096;2108;2120;2132;2144
snake	cobra,yellow trulku of the monkey	1905;1917;1929;1941;1953;1965;1977;1989;2001;2013;2025;2037;2049;2061;2073;2085;2097;2109;2121;2133;2145
horse	lava,red trulku of the sheep	1906;1918;1930;1942;1954;1966;1978;1990;2002;2014;2026;2038;2050;2062;2074;2086;2098;2110;2122;2134;2146
sheep	water spring,black trulku of the horse	1907;1919;1931;1943;1955;1967;1979;1991;2003;2015;2027;2039;2051;2063;2075;2087;2099;2111;2123;2135;2147
monkey	trisagion,stele,marble,green trulku of the snake	1908;1920;1932;1944;1956;1968;1980;1992;2004;2016;2028;2040;2052;2064;2076;2088;2100;2112;2124;2136;2148
rooster	dinosaur gong,yellow trulku of the dragon	1909;1921;1933;1945;1957;1969;1981;1993;2005;2017;2029;2041;2053;2065;2077;2089;2101;2113;2125;2137;2149
dog	mammifer,red trulku of the rabbit	1910;1922;1934;1946;1958;1970;1982;1994;2006;2018;2030;2042;2054;2066;2078;2090;2102;2114;2126;2138;2150
pig	copper,black trulku of the tiger	1911;1923;1935;1947;1959;1971;1983;1995;2007;2019;2031;2043;2055;2067;2079;2091;2103;2115;2127;2139;2151

http://wikimedia.org   www.wikipedia.org/wiki/Category:Female_religious_leaders
http://wikipedia.org http://ro.wikibooks.org http://en.wikipedia.org/wiki/Category:Media
http://wiktionary.org   http://en.wikipedia.org/wiki/Category:World_Wide_Web
http://www.spitalsighet.ro   http://en.wikipedia.org/wiki/Category:Medicine
http://www.tenisclubsighet.ro   http://en.wikipedia.org/wiki/Category:Tennis
www.onelook.com   www.mozilla.com   www.wikipedia.org/wiki/Spelling_reform
www.google.com   www.google.com/language_tools   http://translate.google.com
www.microsoft.com   www.beelinetv.com   www.wikipedia.org/wiki/Woman_imam
www.verbix.com/languages/romanian.shtml   http://es.wikipedia.org/wiki/Rumania
www.wikipedia.org/wiki/Category:Astrology   http://it.wikipedia.org/wiki/Romania
www.wikipedia.org/wiki/Category:Biotechnology   http://sl.wikipedia.org/wiki/Romunija
www.wikipedia.org/wiki/Category:Cardiovascular_system   http://www.wikibooks.org
www.wikipedia.org/wiki/Category:Chromosomes http://cs.wikipedia.org/wiki/Rumunsko
www.wikipedia.org/wiki/Category:Employment   http://sk.wikipedia.org/wiki/Rumunsko
www.wikipedia.org/wiki/Category:Genetics   http://fr.wikipedia.org/wiki/Femme_rabbin
www.wikipedia.org/wiki/Category:Health_effectors   www.wikipedia.org/wiki/Romania
www.wikipedia.org/wiki/Category:Legislatures   http://pt.wikipedia.org/wiki/Romenia
www.wikipedia.org/wiki/Category:Principles   www.wikipedia.org/wiki/Category:Tulkus
www.wikipedia.org/wiki/Category:Reference_works   www.simi.ro   www.gecotv.ro
www.wikipedia.org/wiki/Category:Religion   http://vi.wikipedia.org/wiki/Romania
www.wikipedia.org/wiki/Category:Sighetu_Marmației   www.ms.ro   www.mae.ro
www.wikipedia.org/wiki/Category:Tree_of_life   http://tr.wikipedia.org/wiki/Romanya
www.wikipedia.org/wiki/Category:World_government   www.parlament.ro   www.edu.ro
www.wikipedia.org/wiki/List_of_women_priests   http://fr.wikipedia.org/wiki/Roumanie
www.wikipedia.org/wiki/Maximum_life_span   http://ro.wikipedia.org/wiki/Romania
www.wikipedia.org/wiki/Portal:Contents/Overviews   www.internetpolyglot.com
www.wikipedia.org/wiki/Zodiac   www.wikipedia.org/wiki/Category:Religious_leaders

The Total Final Zodiacal Compatibility

For an ideal zodiacal compatibility between two persons, the 4 parts of the Chinese zodiac (the hour, day, month and year) have to be reciprocally ideal. When we are looking the ideal date, because there are lots, we will choose the dates, with the compatibilities of the other zodiacs and numerologies.

Example:
Someone born in Sighetul Marmației on XI the 24th 1950, standard hour(not being the daylight saving time) 2:10 at night, has the following pillars from the place of birth: Chinese year=tiger M;Chinese month=pig f; Chinese day=pig w; Chinese hour=buffalo w

Now we search for the:
- **ideal Chinese years, then the**
- **ideal Chinese months from the ideal years that were found, after that the**
- **ideal Chinese days from these ideal Chinese months and finally the**
- **ideal Chinese hours from the ideal Chinese days**

These are the dates that have the Chinese year, month, day and hour concomitantly ideal with that of the searcher. We observe that the ideal years can be at big distances and can be without ideal months, some ideal months without ideal days, and some ideal days without ideal hours. We find the year and the day and then the other periods.

The ideal cyclical binomial intervals		
25, 35, rat buffalo, horse sheep	15, 45, monkey snake, tiger pig	5, 55, dragon rooster, dog rabbit
8, 28, 32, rat dragon monkey, buffalo snake rooster, tiger horse dog, rabbit sheep pig		

The standard dates and hours with the **4 pillars from the place of birth** are put in this table, what is **ideal** being **thickened**:

The Chinese pillar of the	XI 24 1950	**III 16 1935**	**III 20 1935**	**XII 28 1935**	**II 11 1942**	**III 3 1942**	**III 15 1958**	**III 19 1958**	**VII 13 1958**	**VII 17 1958**	**VIII 6 1958**
year	tiger M	**pig t**	**pig t**	**pig t**	**horse W**	**horse W**	**dog E**	**dog E**	**dog E**	**dog E**	**dog E**
month	pig f	**rabbit e**	**rabbit e**	rat E	**tiger W**	**tiger W**	**rabbit t**	**rabbit t**	**sheep e**	**sheep e**	**sheep e**
day	pig w	**rabbit m**	**sheep t**	**tiger E**	**sheep t**	**rabbit t**	**rabbit m**	**sheep t**	**rabbit m**	**sheep t**	**rabbit t**
hour	buffalo w (2:10, standard hour, Romania)	**rat E (00-1)**	**snake m (9-11) or rooster t (17-19)**	**rooster m (17-19)**	**snake m (9-11) or rooster t (17-19)**	**snake m (9-11) or rooster t (17-19)**	**rat E (00-1)**	**snake m (9-11) or rooster t (17-19)**	**rat E (00-1)**	**snake m (9-11) or rooster t (17-19)**	**snake m (9-11) or rooster t (17-19)**

XI 24 1950 and XII 28 1935 are the pair.

There can be made numerological grids and calculated the other numbers. We apply the other systems known, for comparisons between these dates and the other shifted ones.

In this example there are the pillars from the place of birth, but there can be calculated also the pillars from Beijing with the introduction of the places of birth of the searched persons.It can be made that both our 4 pillars from the place of birth and our 4 pillars from Beijing to be ideal with the 4 Chinese pillars from the place of birth and the 4 ones from Beijing of the searched persons, by finding the adequate birth time zones, so of the places on Earth that make possible the increase of the compatibilities. When at Beijing only our Chinese hour is changing, there can be found all the 8 ideal pillars in some zones on Earth, but when we advance or regress with one day, already the chances to have all the 8 pillars ideal decrease at Beijing. Thus if it is not possible that all the pillars, both from the place of birth and the pillars from Beijing, to be concomitantly ideal, there are the options:

- all the pillars from the place of birth ideal and the search of the time zones where the pillars from Beijing to be ideal in a bigger proportion too; for this we take all the time zones with the Earth's contained regions, for each standard date and hour that have the pillars from the place of birth ideal and we transform them to the standard time zone from Beijing

- all the pillars from Beijing ideal,that give other ideal dates and hours for the standard time from Beijing,and the search of the time zones,and then,more exactly,of the places of birth on Globe where, also many more pillars from the place of birth, to be ideal

There are also the pillars at each time zone.

With the calculation of all the Chinese pillars we will see that the belonging of the countries and regions to certain time zones is variated, the same the period of the summer time.

Thru calculi, at the free internet addresses mentioned at the classical zodiac, we find that the ascendant is Virgin. The ascendant and the rest of the calculated cusps can also be used for the selection of the ideal Chinese dates. It is looked in which of the ideal Chinese hours, the Ascendant is ideal. We can search also the signs of the Moon's nods, Chiron, Juno and other bodies or points from the sky.

Discussions:
The corals are fixed in general, the shells from a lake or the ocean, don't move according to the compatible zones, the same the algae, the medusas, the marine mammals, but also the fishes are frequently met only in certain oceans. The flowers give seeds with the help of the insects that transport the pollen from a flower to another, these flowers are not born in other periods of the year in order to be compatible after the months' zodiac and neither the majority of the grains of pollen don't get to flowers from another terrestrial compatible zone. The insects live little too, almost all don't travel on long distances, so they do not beneficiate from the compatibilities of the planets Jupiter and Saturn, not living years, and neither from the equilateral triangle's zones, because they do not meet. Many other creatures live little and do not exist in all the parts of the Earth. Yet, the elephants live approximately 60 years(in the Indochina zone: at the Dai people, instead of the pig from the Chinese zodiac is the elephant; the Vietnamese zodiac has instead of the rabbit, the cat, the Birmanese and the Siamese are the most known in the world; and at the Hainanese Li people the first in the cycle is the rooster and the last is the monkey, she is the orangutan who lives, rarely, 60 years), they bring into the world the elephant cub at night, in order to adjust gradually to the solar light, but this means they do not have sometimes the ideal match after the Chinese hour. Many birds fly over seas and countries, but not according to the astrological ideal zones, situated on the west-east direction, but to the heat, on the north-south direction.

In the following tables (the classical zodiacal signs are taken from the ephemeredes tables for the 00 GMT hour, so not transformed, this table being an approximation; thru calculi or on the internet sites we can find the exact degrees and the zodiacal signs); what is **thickened** is the **ideal** for the one that seeks:

	The date of the searcher	The standard dates of the Chinese ideal pillars from the place of birth of the pair or friends									
	XI 24 1950	**III 16** 1935	**III 20** 1935	**XII 28** 1935	II **11** 1942	**III** 3 1942	III 15 **1958**	III **19** **1958**	VII 13 **1958**	VII 17 **1958**	VIII 6 **1958**
Sun	Sagittarius degree 2	Fishes dg 24	Fishes dg 28	Capricorn dg 5	Aquarius dg 22	Fishes dg 12	Fishes dg 24	Fishes dg 28	Cancer dg 20	Cancer dg 24	**Lion** dg 13
Moon	Taurus degree 25	**Leo**	**Virgo** /Libra	Capricorn/ Aquarius	Sagittarius /**Capricorn**	**Virgo** /Libra	Capricorn	Fishes	**Taurus**/ Gemini	Cancer /**Lion**	Aries/ Taurus
Mercury	Sagittarius degree 14	Aquarius dg 26	Fishes dg 1	Capricorn dg 15	Aquarius dg 18 R	Aquarius dg 15	**Aries** dg 4	**Aries** dg 12	**Lion** dg 13	**Lion** dg 18	Virgin dg 7
Venus	Sagittarius degree 4	**Aries** dg 22	**Aries** dg 27	Scorpion dg 22	Aquarius dg 8 R	Aquarius dg 6	Aquarius dg 10	Aquarius dg 13	Gemini dg 19	Gemini dg 23	Cancer dg 17
Mars	Capricorn degree 14	Libra dg 22R	Libra dg 21R	Aquarius dg 16	**Taurus** dg 16	**Taurus** dg 28	Capricorn dg 28	Aquarius dg 1	Aries dg 24	Aries dg 27	**Taurus** dg 9
Jupiter	Aquarius degree 29	Scorpion dg 23R	Scorpion dg 23R	Sagittarius dg 10	**Gemini** dg 11	**Gemini** dg 12	Scorpion **dg 0 R**	Scorpion **dg 0 R**	**Libra** dg 22	**Libra** dg 22	**Libra** dg 24
Saturn	Virgin degree 29	Fishes dg 3	Fishes dg 3	Fishes dg 5	**Taurus** dg 22	**Taurus** dg 23	Sagittarius dg 25	Sagittarius dg 25	Sagittarius dg 20R	Sagittarius dg 20R	Sagittarius dg19 R
Uranus	Cancer degree8R	Aries dg 29	Aries dg 29	Taurus dg 1 R	Taurus dg 26	Taurus dg 26	Lion dg 7 R	Lion dg 7 R	Lion dg 10	Lion dg 10	Lion dg 12
Neptune	Libra degree 18	Virgo dg12 R	Virgo dg12 R	Virgo dg 16	Virgin dg 29 R	Virgin dg 28R	Scorpion dg 4 R	Scorpion dg 4 R	Scorpion dg 2 R	Scorpion dg 2	Scorpion dg 2
Pluto	Lion dg 19 R	Cancer dg 23R	Cancer dg 23R	Cancer dg 26R	Lion dg 4 R	Lion dg 3 R	Virgin dg 0 R	Virgin dg 0 R	Virgin dg 0	Virgin dg 0	Virgin dg 0
ascendant	Virgin dg 28	By searching the places of birth, we find if the Chinese hours pillars are the ideal ascendants **Aries dg 1, Taurus dg 28** or **Capricorn dg 28**.									

In the table: R=retrograde (because the zodiacal signs are seen from Earth, it seems that a planet on the sky goes backwards, but in fact planets don't go backwards. If we would be in the center of the Sun almost nothing would appear retrograde, but there are still points, comets and all the other stars and galaxies, that would still seem to go backwards sometimes, so retrograde, even from the Sun. The essential is that on the zodiacal circle it is in that zodiacal sign and in that degree, <u>the explanation for the retrograde would be the introspection</u>)

The solar system	Sun	Mercury	Venus	Moon	Earth	Mars	Jupiter	Saturn	Uranus	Neptune	Pluto
The period of rotation around its own axis	25 days	59 days	243 days	27 days	24 hours	24 hours	10 hours	10 hours	17 R hours	16 hours	6 days
The period of rotation around the center	250 million years	88 days	225 days	27 days	365 days	687 days	12 years	30 years	84 years	165 years	248 years

Considering that a Chinese animal begins at the 15 degree of the classical zodiac sign (this time its symbol is put), we can see (also to choose the ideal date, thru the compatibility of the animals) the next table; the Chinese animal between the brackets does not belong to the Chinese pillars, not being the binomial element, but it is a theoretical overlap of it on the classical zodiac signs; the **ideal** dates, the ideal Chinese animals and the ideal symbols of the classical signs are **thickened**:

	The date of the searcher	The standard dates of the Chinese ideal pillars from the place of birth of the pair or friends									
	XI 24 1950	**III 16 1935**	**III 20 1935**	**XII 28 1935**	**II 11 1942**	**III 3 1942**	**III 15 1958**	**III 19 1958**	**VII 13 1958**	**VII 17 1958**	**VIII 6 1958**
destiny number	5	**1**	5	7	2	**4**	5	**9**	7	2	**1**
Sun	♐ degree 2 (pig)	♓ dg 24 (rabbit)	♓ dg 28 (rabbit)	♑ dg 5 (rat)	♒ dg 22 (tiger)	♓ dg 12 (tiger)	♓ dg 24 (rabbit)	♓ dg 28 (rabbit)	♋ dg 20 (sheep)	♋ dg 24 (sheep)	♌ dg 13 (sheep)
Moon	♉ dg 25 (snake)	♌ (sheep)	♍/♎ (rooster)	♑/♒ (buffalo)	♐/♑ (rat)	♍/♎ (monkey /rooster)	♑/♒ (buffalo)	♓ (rabbit)	♉/♊ (snake/ horse)	♋/♌ (sheep)	♈/♉ (dragon)
Mercury	♐ degree 14 (pig)	♒ dg 26 (tiger)	♓ dg 1 (tiger)	♑ dg 15 (buffalo)	♒ dg 18R (tiger)	♒ dg 15 (tiger)	♈ dg 4 (rabbit)	♈ dg 12 (rabbit)	♌ dg 13 (sheep)	♌ dg 18 (monkey)	♍ dg 7 (monkey)
Venus	♐ degree 4 (pig)	♈ dg 22 (dragon)	♈ dg 27 (dragon)	♍ dg 22 (pig)	♒ dg 8 R (buffalo)	♒ dg 6 (buffalo)	♒ dg 10 (buffalo)	♒ dg 13 (buffalo)	♊ dg 19 (horse)	♊ dg 23 (horse)	♋ dg 17 (sheep)
Mars	♑ degree 14 (rat)	♎ dg 22R (dog)	♎ dg 21R (dog)	♒ dg 16 (tiger)	♉ dg 16 (snake)	♉ dg 28 (snake)	♑ dg 28 (buffalo)	♒ dg 1 (buffalo)	♈ dg 24 (dragon)	♈ dg 27 (dragon)	♉ dg 9 (dragon)
Jupiter	♒ degree 29 (tiger)	♏ dg 23R (pig)	♏ dg 23R (pig)	♐ dg 10 (pig)	♊ dg 11 (snake)	♊ dg 12 (snake)	♏ dg 0 R (dog)	♏ dg 0 R (dog)	♎ dg 22 (dog)	♎ dg 22 (dog)	♎ dg 24 (dog)
Saturn	♍ degree 29 (rooster)	♓ dg 3 (tiger)	♓ dg 3 (tiger)	♓ dg 5 (dragon)	♉ dg 22 (snake)	♉ dg 23 (snake)	♐ dg 25 (rat)	♐ dg 25 (rat)	♐ dg 20R (rat)	♐ dg 20R (rat)	♐ dg 19 R (rat)
Uranus	♋ dg 8 R (horse)	♈ dg 29 (dragon)	♈ dg 29 (dragon)	♉ dg 1 R (dragon)	♉ dg 26 (snake)	♉ dg 26 (snake)	♌ dg 7 R (sheep)	♌ dg 7 R (sheep)	♌ dg 10 (sheep)	♌ dg 10 (sheep)	♌ dg 12 (sheep)
Neptune	♎ dg 18 (dog)	♍ dg12R (rooster)	♍ dg12 R (rooster)	♍ dg 16 (rooster)	♍ dg 29R (rooster)	♍ dg 28R (rooster)	♏ dg 4 R (dog)	♏ dg 4 R (dog)	♏ dg 2 R (dog)	♏ dg 2 (dog)	♏ dg 2 (dog)
Pluto	♌ dg 19 R (monkey)	♋ dg 23R (sheep)	♋ dg 23R (sheep)	♋ dg 26R (sheep)	♌ dg 4 R (sheep)	♌ dg 3 R (sheep)	♍ dg 0 R (monkey)	♍ dg 0 R (monkey)	♍ dg 0 (monkey)	♍ dg 0 (monkey)	♍ dg 0 (monkey)
ascendant	♍ dg 28 (rooster)	By searching the places of birth, we find if the Chinese hours pillars are the ideal ascendants **(dragon)♈/♉**, **(serpent)♉** or **(buffalo)♑/♒**.									

The Analysis and the Predictions upon Life

By comparing the dates of an event, the birth dates of some persons, we can find the influence of zodiacs and numbers in the:
-past
-present
-future

The prediction can be:

- hourly (by comparing the Chinese hour of birth with the Chinese hour from that day; the comparison of our ascendant of the classical zodiac with the ascendants of that day)

- daily (the Chinese day of birth with the wanted Chinese day from the desired date, the number of the day, the zodiacal sign of the Moon)

- weekly, monthly (the Chinese month; thru the solar, mercurian, venusian, marsian zodiacal signs; the number of the month; the calendar month)

- annually (the Chinese year, the jupiterian, saturnian zodiacal sign; the number of the year)

- on many years, decenniums, centuries (like the uranian, neptunian, plutonian zodiac signs)

- on millenniums, eras or an infinite duration (the two vernal points given with the ecliptic; the zodiacal signs of the stars, nebulas, galaxies, universes)

- at any time over any period (by cumulating all the numerologies, zodiacs, decades, degrees, minutes, seconds of the zodiacal signs)

The influence of the Sun on us we see it and know it, thru the seasons that it determines, through the ultraviolet rays that fix the calcium into the bone, that can cause skin cancer, remissions in psoriasis or the strengthening of the psychic system. The influence of the Moon can be seen thru the tides created daily, these are due to the forces of attraction between the Moon and the Earth, that are also between all the celestial bodies and us.

We will always find a particle, an asteroid, a planetoid, a star, a constellation, a galaxy or anything else that is for us in a zodiacal sign.

The Conclusions of the Zodiacal Compatibilities

The moment of birth was studied thru a multitude of zodiacs and numerologies.
All are based upon:
- mythologies from different parts of the Earth
- experimentation
- imagination
- and mostly the desire to know the universe
These are offering us perspectives on psychology, the sentiments and the education.

İnglând, the country formed of all the countries of the world, with İngliş, the human native language.

> **- biometrical acts with the official hour of birth, this is written for the first time in the registers of births from the hospitals**
> **- web:**
> > **- the place, hour of birth**
> > **- the day, month and year of birth on the search engine**
> > **- data**

The zodiacal signs have an explanation: the energies from the universe reach directly the baby at the moment of the birth, stumbling themselves on galaxies, stars (the closest being the Sun), planets (the closest are the planets that rotate around the Sun), satellites (the closest, from Earth, being the Moon), planetoids, asteroids and other particles. There are also other zodiacs that begin from the moment of conception.

In the future, when we will populate also satellites, planets, galaxies, universes, the universe, our earthly astrological system on a planet, where a day would be of 300 earthly days, and a night, of 200 earthly days, that would rotate itself around a sun in 500 earthly days and that would have other 4 suns and 5 satellites, will be analyzed. On Terra, from the poles to the polar circle, the solar light lasts for entire days till half a year, and the night, in the rest of the year; there the yin(night) and yang(day) daily principles, the equinoxes and the solstices (given also in the trees zodiac) stand up by imaginative transfer from the places where these exist.

The binomial years affinity					
Animals	Elements				
yang yin	Tree earth	Fire metal	Earth water	Metal tree	Water fire
rat buffalo	1924;1984;2044;2104;2164 1949;2009;2069;2129;2189	1936;1996;2056;2116;2176 1901;1961;2021;2081;2141	1948;2008;2068;2128;2188 1913;1973;2033;2093;2153	1900;1960;2020;2080;2140 1925;1985;2045;2105;2165	1912;1972;2032;2092;2152 1937;1997;2057;2117;2177
dragon rooster	1904;1964;2024;2084;2144 1909;1969;2029;2089;2149	1916;1976;2036;2096;2156 1921;1981;2041;2101;2161	1928;1988;2048;2108;2168 1933;1993;2053;2113;2173	1940;2000;2060;2120;2180 1945;2005;2065; 2125;2185	1952;2012;2072;2132;2192 1957;2017;2077;2137;2197
monkey snake	1944;2004;2064;2124;2184 1929;1989;2049;2109;2169	1956;2016;2076;2136;2196 1941;2001;2061;2121;2181	1908;1968;2028;2088;2148 1953;2013;2073;2133;2193	1920;1980;2040;2100;2160 1905;1965;2025;2085;2145	1932;1992;2052;2112;2172 1917;1977;2037;2097;2157
tiger pig	1914;1974;2034;2094;2154 1959;2019;2079;2139;2199	1926;1986;2046;2106;2166 1911;1971;2031;2091;2151	1938;1998;2058;2118;2178 1923;1983;2043;2103;2163	1950;2010;2070;2130;2190 1935;1995;2055;2115;2175	1902;1962;2022;2082;2142 1947;2007;2067;2127;2187
horse sheep	1954;2014;2074;2134;2194 1919;1979;2039;2099;2159	1906;1966;2026;2086;2146 1931;1991;2051;2111;2171	1918;1978;2038;2098;2158 1943;2003;2063;2123;2183	1930;1990;2050;2110;2170 1955;2015;2075;2135;2195	1942;2002;2062;2122;2182 1907;1967;2027;2087;2147
dog rabbit	1934;1994;2054;2114;2174 1939;1999;2059;2119;2179	1946;2006;2066;2126;2186 1951;2011;2071;2131;2191	1958;2018;2078;2138;2198 1903;1963;2023;2083;2143	1910;1970;2030;2090;2150 1915;1975;2035;2095;2155	1922;1982;2042;2102;2162 1927;1987;2047;2107;2167

Closure

all are contained one in the other

|

the plants and the animals started from a cell and other forms of organization of
the matter
found in stars, planets, asteroids and in space

|

this, from components
(proteins, lipids, glucoses, marine salts…)

|

these, from elements

|

that are composed of different particles, as are
the electrons, that orbit around the centre,
like the planets rotate themselves around a star

|

each particle being constituted from an infinity of particles
(there are two directions: the first one, to the infinite interior
of any particle, thus being an infinity of interior universes, and
the second one, to the unlimited exterior of the particle, the
exterior universe, that contains all the interior universes)

|

all being
(religion, zodiac, philosophy, science)
God
Mother Father
Child

Bibliography

Omraam Mikhael Aivanhov – Zodiacul cheie a omului şi a universului (Le zodiaque,
  clé de l'homme et de l'univers) – Editura Prosveta, România
Michael Angles, Siavoch Darakchan, Mian Shen Zhu – Suflul şi energia Qi Gong
  (Souffle et énergie. Le Qi Gong) – Editura Polirom, România, 2001
Minunata lume a animalelor (Wildlife Explorer) – International Masters Publishers, România
Rodford Barrat – Elemente de numerologie (The Elements of Numerology) –
  Editura Teora, România, 2001
Anatol Basarab – Numerologia în viaţa fiecăruia – Editura Miracol, România, 1999
Valer Butura – Enciclopedie de etnobotanică românească – Editura Şti. şi Enciclopedică, România, 1979
Teodor, Teodora Cabar – Particularităţi în patologia meridianelor – Editura All, România, 1998
Anca Maria Christodorescu – Dicţionar român-francez – Editura Gramar, România, 1996
Dan Ciupercă – Astrologia în noua eră – Editura Safire, România, 1994
Armand Constantinescu – Cer şi destin – Editura Icar, România, 1999
Adrian Cotrobescu – Astrologia practică – Editura Teora, România, 2002
Mircea Duduleanu – Munca reflectată în proverbele lumii,proverbe universale – Editura Albatros, România
Bernard Dumpleton – Descoperiţi minunile lumii (Discovering the Wonders of Our World) – Editura
  Reader's Digest, România, 2004
Jorg Eikmann – Personalitatea grupelor sanguine (Was die Blutgruppe verrat) –
  Editura Gemma Print, România, 2004
Mircea Eliade – Morfologia religiilor (Traité d'histoire des religions) – Editura
  Jurnalul Literar, România, 1993
Mircea Eliade, Ioan Culianu – Dicţionar al religiilor (Dictionnaire des religions,
  The Eliade Guide to World Religions) – Editura Humanitas, România, 1993
George Lăzărescu – Dicţionar de mitologie – Editura Ion Creangă, România, 1979
Leon Leviţchi, Andrei Bantaş – Dicţionar englez-român – Editura Teora, România, 1993
Gaudin Philippe – Marile religii (Les grandes religions) – Editura Orizonturi, România,1995
Llewellyn Georg – Horoscopul de la A la Z (Llewellyn's new A to Z Horoscope) –
  Editura Polirom, România, 2006
Dorian Green – Zodiac universal – Editura Vremea, România, 1999
Mandics Gyorgy – Civilizaţia şi culturile Africii vechi – Editura Sport-Turism, România, 1983
Gheorghina Haneş – Dicţionar francez-român român-francez – Editura Ştiinţifică, România,1974
Raza Kapoor – Ayurveda tratat de terapie – Editura L.V.B., România, 1999
Hermann Kinder, Werner Hilgemann – Atlas de istorie mondială (Atlas Weltgeschichte,
  Atlas of World History) – Editura Rao, România, 2001
Gabriel Mihailovici – ABC-ul astrologiei – Editura Tipo, România, 1995
James Muirden – Notre univers – Hatier, France, 1985
Tudor Opriş – Din tainele lumii vii animale, plante – Editura Didactică şi Pedagogică, România, 1992
Irina Panovf – Romanian-English-Romanian Dictionary – Editura Ştiinţifică şi Enci., România, 1982
Ileana Pârlea,Cristina Ştefănescu,Léauté – La naissance de Rome – Editura Prietenii Cărţii, România, 1993
Michele Perras – Incursiune în astronumerologie (Astro-numérologie pratique) –
  Editura Polirom, România, 2001
Jon Sandifer – Astrologie fengshui pentru o viaţă în armonie (Feng Shui Astrology
  Using 9 Star Ki to Achieve Harmony and Happiness) – Editura Polirom , România, 2004
Claire Savard – Palma, numerele şi destinul (À la recherche du partenaire idéal par la
  chirologie et la numérologie) – Editura Polirom, România, 2000
Xing Shu – Horoscopul chinezesc – Editura Gemma Press, România, 2000
Theofil Simenschy – Un dicţionar al înţelepciunii – Editura Junimea, România, 1979
Jean Simpson – Hot Numbers – Gramercy Books, America, 1998
Mihaela Slăvescu – Dicţionar francez-român – Editura Gramar, România, 1995
Richard Smith, Takeo Mori – Zodiacul japonez – Editura Marathon, România, 1994
Sheila Snowden – Le jeune astronome – Editions G.P., France, 1983
Neill Sommerville – Perechea ideală după zodiacul chinezesc (What's Your Chinese
  Love Sign) – Editura Lider, România, 1999
Cristina Vanea – Horoscopul chinezesc 2000 – România
Olenka de Veer – Mini-encyclopedie de l'astrologie – Loisir, France, 1984
Victor Vostokov – Incursiune în medicina indo-tibetană – Editura Polirom, România, 2001
Liu Xiang – Marele horoscop chinezesc – Editura Lucman, România

Internet

http://en.wikipedia.org/wiki/List_of_social_networking_websites   www.sighet.net
http://pages.infinit.net/histoire/calendrier.html http://en.wikipedia.org/wiki/Online_chat
http://webexhibits.org   www.zodii.ro   www.wikipedia.org/wiki/List_of_sportspeople
www.astro-france.com   http://en.wikipedia.org/wiki/Lists_of_people_by_occupation
www.doublesign.com www.fidelia.ro www.wikipedia.org/wiki/List_of_search_engines
www.e-sighet.ro   www.sighet-online.ro   www.primaria-sighet.ro   www.marmatia.ro
www.findastrologer.com www.wikipedia.org/wiki/Category:Books www.asiaflash.com
www.imdb.com/search www.louisg.net www.geomancy.net/astrology/astro/astro.htm
www.nightwing.awebspider.com/correspondance.htm   www.sighet.ro/link.htm
www.tuvy.com/entertainment/chinese_horoscope.htm   www.sighetu-marmatiei.com

Finding out for free the **Chinese pillars** (we don't obtain the results directly with the official hour and date, but after the calculation of the standard hour and date at the place of birth, at Beijing and at the other time zones):
www.fourpillars.net/online4p.php
www.chineseastrologyonline.com/CFTCal2.htm

Finding out our **classical signs** and cusps of the houses (here it can be introduced the official hour and date because the transformation takes place automatically):
www.astro.com
www.astro-software.com
www.0800-horoscope.com/birthchart.php

Finding some **numbers** of the date of birth and of the name:
www.numerology-guide.com
www.sun-angel.com/numerology

Finding the **pair or friends** on internet addresses:
        on http://google.com the searched date of birth and the internet address
http://trova-amici.alice.it   www.care2.com   www.cyworld.com   www.date4u.be
www.amoureux.com www.skyrock.com www.circle.pk www.tribe.net www.trilulilu.ro
www.blogtv.com   www.sentimente.ro   www.neogen.ro   www.livejournal.com
www.clopotel.ro www.icq.com   www.couchsurfing.com www.cirip.ro www.4ppl.com
www.doctornetworking.com www.stumbleupon.com www.220.ro www.spaces.live.com
www.hi5.com   www.medicalmingle.com   www.a2lavie.com   www.accentdating.com
www.imbee.com www.bebo.com www.fropper.com www.lulu.com www.yepla.com
www.katext.info   www.fanbox.com   www.linkedin.com   www.dontstayin.com
www.lankainternet.com www.orkut.com www.esnips.com www.xing.com www.sibir.ro
www.meetup.com   www.vkontakte.ru   www.piqniq.jp   www.nativenetwork.org
www.netlog.com www.studivz.net www.magnify.net www.ingeri.ro www.friendster.com
www.nexopia.com   www.leclubdes15.com   www.youtube.com   www.facebook.com
www.wasabi.com   www.blogster.com   www.myyearbook.com   www.star104.net
www.weblog.ro   www.multiply.com www.nab.com www.ning.com www.renren.com

My addresses:
http://zhoroscop.hi5.com
http://profiles.yahoo.com/zhoroscop
www.clopotel.ro/zhoroscop
www.myspace.com/zhoroscop